THE KENNEDY
CABINET

THE KENNEDY CABINET

America's Men of Destiny

Deane and David Heller

Foreword by
The Honorable A. S. Mike Monroney
U. S. Senator from Oklahoma

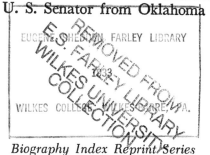

Biography Index Reprint Series

BOOKS FOR LIBRARIES PRESS
FREEPORT, NEW YORK

E 8 4 1
H 4

INTERNATIONAL STANDARD BOOK NUMBER:
0-8369-8002-6

LIBRARY OF CONGRESS CATALOG CARD NUMBER:
77-101829

PRINTED IN THE UNITED STATES OF AMERICA

FOREWORD

Do you have any ideas on achieving peace in Laos or eliminating Communism in Cuba? What would you do about unemployment? Or the outflow of gold? How do you decide which expensive military missile is the best?

These were only a few of the big problems the incoming Cabinet members found waiting for them on the New Frontier. As the secretaries of huge government departments, they were expected to have ideas on these questions of policy even as they faced the usual administrative problems of inspiring loyalty and dedication to duty among thousands of subordinates.

Deane and David Heller have given us a lively account of the men chosen by President Kennedy to be members of his Cabinet and head the departments which together with the office of the Presidency constitute the Executive Branch of the Federal Government.

They were selected after the most methodical and intensive search, led personally by the President. His success in discovering and attracting men of ability and energy is now well known. I have heard some of the Administration's severest critics in the Senate express unqualified admiration for the Cabinet.

In a few short months we have seen serious problems faced with cool reason and firm decision. We have heard stories of burning midnight oil, surprise visits to obscure offices, and informal meetings with career employees who had rarely seen former department heads. In fact, the combination of long hours and new personal responsibility is making life for some on the New Frontier almost as rugged as it once was on the Old Frontier of the West.

As in the first days of the New Deal, Washington is once again the focus of exciting ideas and opportunities for achievement, and, of course, personal recognition. The new Cabinet members have not accepted the view that service in the Government is a dull burden or a personal sacrifice. They came with enthusiasm, seeing a great opportunity to help improve the present and influence the future of our own Nation and of the whole world.

Mr. and Mrs. Heller have caught this spirit, especially in their reports of interviews with the members of the Cabinet. Practical idealism is evident in the character of each man. It is a quality pleasing to all Americans, and I know it will give this book a special appeal for students scanning the future for challenge.

A. S Mike Monroney
United States Senate

NOTE

United States Senator A. S. Mike Monroney of Oklahoma is one of the most distinguished and universally respected members of the Senate. A graduate of the University of Oklahoma, Senator Monroney was a distinguished newspaperman with the Scripps-Howard newspaper system before being elected to Congress in 1938.

He served twelve years in the House of Representatives and was the winner of the coveted Collier's Award for Distinguished Congressional Service in 1945. He is co-author, with the late Senator Robert M. LaFollette, of the legislative reorganization bill of 1946. He was elected to the United States Senate in 1950 and was re-elected in 1956.

CHAPTER ONE

Attorney General Robert Kennedy
and the Department of Justice

THE OFFICE——The Attorney General, who presides over the Department of Justice, is the nation's chief legal officer and one of the most important officials in the federal government. He heads the "largest law office in the world." More than 31,000 attorneys, investigators, law enforcement officers and others work for this department.

There are thirteen divisions to the Justice Department, the most famous of which is the Federal Bureau of Investigation. Others include the Office of the Solicitor General and the Office of Legal Counsel; the Office of Alien Property; the Tax, Civil, Lands, Anti-Trust, Criminal, Civil Rights, and Internal Security Divisions; the Bureau of Prisons, the Immigration and Naturalization Service, and the United States Marshals and United States Attorneys.

As a member of the President's Cabinet, the Attorney General is the chief legal adviser to the President and the chief law enforcement officer of the federal government. He construes the laws under which the Executive Department operates. He furnishes legal advice in all federal cases. The Attorney General and his staff review the legality of all Executive Orders of the President and draft legislation at the behest of the President.

As the chief law enforcement officer of the federal government, the Attorney General deals with such touchy subjects as civil rights, tax and antitrust prosecutions; prosecutions for federal crimes such as kidnaping, counterfeiting, narcotics violations, perjury charges, espionage, labor racketeering and subversion.

The Attorney General also supervises the administration of the Department of Justice; directs special matters relating to national defense; directs twenty-eight penal institutions, ranging from training schools for juvenile delinquents, and jails and camps to penitentiaries and the famous Alcatraz; supervises the work of United States Attorneys and their assistants, and United States Marshals, and deputy Marshals; approves abstracts of title for lands acquired by the government for national parks, slum clearance projects, post office sites and such installations as air fields, camp sites and naval bases; supervises all litigation in the courts, civil or criminal, to which the government is a party; represents the United States in legal matters generally; appears in the Supreme Court of the United States in cases of exceptional importance; and provides special counsel for the United States in certain cases or when the character of the interests involved requires such action. (These are only a few of the major duties of the Attorney General.)

He is, as you can see, a busy man!

The post of Attorney General was created by the Judiciary Act of 1789. Edmund Randolph of Virginia, a close friend and confidant of President George Washington, was the first Attorney General. Robert Kennedy is the sixty-fourth. Mr. Randolph's salary was $1,500 per year. Mr. Kennedy's is $25,000. Poor Mr. Randolph, the first Attorney General, also had to furnish his own office, stationery, legal books and law clerk out of his salary!

The Justice Department today occupies an entire city block between Ninth and Tenth Streets and Washington's famed Pennsylvania and Constitution Avenues.

THE MAN——Perhaps the most interesting member of the President's entire Cabinet—from the standpoint of personality and controversy—is Attorney General Robert F. Kennedy.

A celebrated crime and labor racket investigator and manager of his brother's successful races for Congress, the Senate and the Presidency, Robert Kennedy is also the only brother of a President ever to sit in the Cabinet.

Despite the fact that, as the winning candidate's campaign manager, Robert Kennedy could naturally have expected a Cabinet seat almost as a matter of course, the fact that he was also the President's brother caused his appointment to attract widespread praise as well as criticism.

U. S. partisan politics being what they are, Robert Kennedy's appointment was a "natural" for Republicans to de-

nounce. Some were particularly vehement because they recalled the younger Kennedy as a rough and tough critic of
the Justice Department under GOP Attorneys General, lash-
ing it for "inaction" and "incompetence."

Critics were numerous and vocal. U. S. Senator Gordon
Allot, Colorado Republican, harshly denounced the younger
Kennedy on the Senate floor as "unqualified." "Nepotism"
and "favoritism" were words heard by anti-Kennedyites.
Someone invented a gibe that the President's initials, JFK,
stood for "Jobs For Kinfolk."

Considerable grumbling came from some members of the
traditionally conservative American Bar Association. This
centered around two points: (1) Robert Kennedy's legal experience had been exclusively with the federal government,
and (2) he had no experience as a trial lawyer.

The writers asked a past president of the American Bar
Association (who prefers to remain anonymous) why he so
objected to the younger Kennedy's appointment.

"He's never argued a court case in his life," snorted the
attorney, an internationally famous lawyer, with considerable
heat.

"Don't you think he'll make a good Attorney General?" we
asked.

The former American Bar Association president considered
this.

"Yes," he said grudgingly, "he'll make a good Attorney
General. In fact, he'll make the best Attorney General we've
had since Homer Cummings" (a former Attorney General
under President Franklin D. Roosevelt).

"Then why are you so against him?"

The lawyer, a man in his late fifties who has held numerous
high government posts, grimly thought about the matter in
frustration. "I suppose I really haven't got any good reason,"
he admitted. Then he added defiantly: "But I am."

Of course, Robert Kennedy supporters are just as voluble
and far more numerous than his critics. Highly respected
United States Senator John McClellan, Robert Kennedy's
chief on the famous McClellan Committee, fervently declared
that the younger Kennedy has "superb qualities of administrative and executive leadership" and that "his professional skill
as a lawyer has not been excelled by anyone I have seen in
my twenty-two years in Congress."

The Washington *Daily News,* which vigorously opposed
John Kennedy for President, applauded the selection of

9

Robert Kennedy as Attorney General. Among knowledgeable people in Washington, it is hard to find many who do not think he will make an outstanding Attorney General.

One person who is not worried on this count is the President himself. Reminded that his appointment of his brother was without historical precedent, President Kennedy grinned and stated: "We're going to start a new precedent right now."

Columnist Peter Edson reported a quip of the President's relating to his brother's appointment. Speaking before the Alfalfa Club, he grinningly remarked: "I don't see anything wrong with giving Bobby a little legal experience before he starts practicing law!"

Robert Kennedy, of course, is well aware of the controversy his appointment caused. He is working with a dedicated, almost grim intensity to make an outstanding record.

"Robert Kennedy is a man on the spot. Because of his youth and his relationship with the President, he has to be three times as good as anybody who's ever held this job before—and he will be!"

The confident words were those of a close co-worker and friend of the nation's second-youngest Attorney General. Mr. Kennedy is 35. Robert Rush of Pennsylvania was 34 when named Attorney General in 1814.

When the writers interviewed Attorney General Kennedy in preparation for writing this book, they saw good evidence of why he is regarded as the hardest-driving man in Washington.

At six-thirty in the evening, as the writers were ushered through a suite of rooms into his elaborate private office, a galaxy of secretaries and assistants were working feverishly. It seemed not to have occurred to anybody that it was mealtime, let alone quitting time.

We were curious to see the Attorney General's office. Once it was whimsically described by Byron "Whizzer" White, Deputy Attorney General and former All-American football player, as so large that "you'd need the wind at your back to punt a football from end to end."

Although the office was impressive, Mr. White's remark was obviously made in jest. The president of many a medium-sized U. S. corporation has offices far more lavish. On a table behind his desk reposes a small bust of Lincoln, and on a near-by table stands a color photograph of the President, obviously taken while he was holding a news conference. A model of an early New England sailing ship sits near by.

We were slightly startled to be greeted by the Attorney General in shirt sleeves. The famous Kennedy mop of hair was slightly rumpled. The infectious Kennedy smile was in evidence. A mountain of work seemed to be piled on Mr. Kennedy's desk and on the tables about him. We felt that it was a revealing and significant picture.

Perhaps the bust of Lincoln had something to do with it, but the authors had a momentary impression that they had interrupted a hard-working man who had taken off his coat and was about to split rails and would be doing so again upon our departure. As taxpayers, it was not displeasing to see a public official of such high rank—the brother of the President—so totally immersed in his work.

"Nobody I've ever seen works the way he does," one of his assistants told the writers. "He comes in about nine-thirty in the morning and he often doesn't leave until ten at night. And he usually takes a brief case full of work with him."

Robert Kennedy is as full of repressed energy as a coiled spring. He is also a man with a pleasant smile, great charm and an utter lack of pretense. Above all, he projects an aura of competence and almost limitless determination.

It was this kind of determination, one reflects, which led him, as a smallish, 150-pounder, to make the varsity football team at Harvard and play successfully against the behemoths of modern football. (Incidentally, it was Robert Kennedy's football career which led to the Kennedy family's celebrated enthusiasm for touch football—an enthusiasm which members of the family insist has been greatly exaggerated by the press.)

Robert Kennedy is a born athlete. He swims, skis, water skis, toboggans with his family on their McLean, Virginia, estate and indulges in just about all participation sports. He often exercises in the Justice Department gymnasium in games of handball or volleyball. One of his favorite gifts is a football—given to him by the Baltimore Colts football club.

"What areas will be of special interest to you as Attorney General?" the writers asked Mr. Kennedy.

"We will be very active in three fields," he replied. "In civil rights, in the criminal field, and in antitrust work."

The matter of organized crime has long concerned Robert Kennedy. It was, of course, as a relentless investigator into corruption in the Teamsters' Union that Robert Kennedy first achieved fame. The downfall of Dave Beck, former Teamster President, dates from this Kennedy-directed in-

11

quiry. The celebrated Robert Kennedy–James Hoffa feud dates from the famous Senate investigation which held millions glued to their television sets day after day. Mr. Kennedy has often described Hoffa as "a national menace."

If there are, indeed, the skeletons in the Hoffa closet which Mr. Kennedy believes, it must give the Teamster President some uneasy moments to reflect that he has such a relentless and implacable foe in such a powerful position.

Once, while investigating Teamster corruption, Robert Kennedy was foiled by the problem of a missing witness, whom he had reason to believe had been murdered. A tip was received that the body was buried in an Illinois cornfield. Mr. Kennedy went personally to the supposed spot and, wielding the shovel himself, sought to uncover the "body" himself. Nothing was found.

There is every indication that the Attorney General's thoughts regarding Mr. James Hoffa have not changed an iota since assuming office. In his book, *The Enemy Within,* he states, "A man with Hoffa's power and position and so corrupt, cannot survive in a democratic society if democracy itself is going to survive."

Growing out of this concern, undoubtedly, is the present study in the Justice Department on strengthening federal laws over union funds. There is reportedly $300 million in the health and welfare fund of the Central Conference of Teamsters, and allegedly much of this is under the personal control of James Hoffa.

Attorney General Kennedy has asked Congress for eight new laws aimed against big-time crime. His new ideas aim at making interstate travel illegal if it advances illegal business activities; at strengthening the Firearms Act; and in furthering legislation to "extend the immunity statutes." This would give witnesses who co-operate with government officials in the war on crime more protection and should induce smaller malefactors to co-operate in the successful prosecution of bigger violators.

Attorney General Kennedy also expressed a hope that new legislation would make "more feasible the deporting of criminals who came to this country illegally." Present laws make deportation of criminals born abroad very complex and time-consuming. New plans call for strengthening and expanding the work of the department's Criminal Division.

Five of the other new laws sought by the Attorney General are intended to interfere with the flow of gambling informa-

12

tion and gambling equipment across state lines and to broaden other areas of racketeering control by the FBI. The whole anti-crime legislative program is aimed at giving the federal government increased jurisdiction "in the common battle against the rackets," in the words of the Attorney General. Senator John J. McClellan, head of the Government Operations Committee, told newsmen that he intends to "co-ordinate" future crime investigations with the drive announced by Attorney General Kennedy against leaders of the underworld.

"Would you please comment on the other areas which will be of special concern to you?" we asked Mr. Kennedy.

With his unhurried smile, he replied, with a slight but pleasant accent that could have come from nowhere else but Boston: "We will very vigorously enforce the antitrust laws. There will be inquiries into price-fixing and into mergers of larger groups which will put smaller companies out of business. We will examine very carefully all mergers of large business companies. We will be active in the antitrust field."

Mr. Kennedy paused a moment. Lawyer-like, he chose his words with care and used them with precision.

"I think civil rights will be more difficult," he said, "because it is both more emotional and more explosive. We will work vigorously in civil rights."

There have been rumors that the Attorney General's stay in the Cabinet might be shortened because he might run for Senator or Governor of Massachusetts in 1962.

"Have you given any thought to running for elective office?"

With a smile, Mr. Kennedy shook his head. "Not really," he said. "Perhaps sometime. . ." The writers were left with the impression that the eventuality would be in the very remote future—if at all. Obviously, other things were far more in the Attorney General's mind.

Robert Kennedy, like his brother the President, has worked as a newspaperman, a foreign correspondent, and is the author of the best-selling book, *The Enemy Within.* He is donating all of the royalties from this book to charities for mentally retarded children.

Since his newspaper and writing career is a relatively little-known area of his life, the writers asked him about it.

"I covered the signing of the Japanese Peace Treaty at San Francisco in 1955," he said. "In other trips, I traveled through Russia and the Middle East. My foreign corresponding for the Boston *Post* began in 1947, when I wrote articles on the impending war between Israel and the Arab states. I predicted that Israel would win the war and would maintain itself as a state—even though it was outnumbered. I also went to Berlin to write about the Berlin Airlift."

Robert Kennedy reports that his interest in a government career was initiated by his father and mother. "My father, in particular, felt that the family had done well in America," he said, "and he emphasized that we owed a responsibility of service to the country.

Robert Kennedy's service to his country began during World War II. He was enrolled in a reserve officers' training program when his eldest brother, Joseph P. Kennedy, Jr., a flier, was killed in action. The Navy named a destroyer after him. Robert Kennedy came to Washington, obtained an interview with Secretary of the Navy James Forrestal, and got permission to serve aboard the *Joseph P. Kennedy, Jr.,* as a seaman.

Robert Kennedy's professional career as an attorney has all been with the government. He took his prelegal training at Harvard, then graduated from the University of Virginia Law School. After graduation, he took a job with the Criminal Division of the Department of Justice.

He left the Justice Department after eight months to manage his brother's first campaign for the Massachusetts Senate in 1952. The Kennedy blitz against the then incumbent, firmly entrenched United States Senator Henry Cabot Lodge is part of the folklore of Massachusetts politics. President Eisenhower carried the state by a 211,000 vote plurality against Adlai Stevenson, but John Kennedy stunned the political dopesters by defeating Senator Lodge by 71,000 votes. Behind the scenes, substantial credit was attributed to the tireless work of Campaign Manager Robert Kennedy.

Robert Kennedy then took a job on the vastly publicized Permanent Subcommittee on Investigations—better known as the "McCarthy Committee." He left in 1954 after a celebrated imbroglio with Chief Counsel Roy Cohn. According to newspaper accounts of the time, Robert Kennedy and Cohn almost came to blows. Certainly, there was long-standing friction between the two. The immediate cause of the break was reportedly the threat of Mr. Cohn to "get" Senator Henry M. Jackson, a close friend of Robert Kennedy, who had publicly ridiculed a plan for anti-Communist psychological warfare prepared by Army Private G. David Schine.

Before leaving, Robert Kennedy informed Chairman Mc-

14

Carthy that he felt the committee was headed for "disaster."

When the election of 1954 gave the Democrats a majority in the Senate, Senator John McClellan replaced McCarthy as chairman of the committee and Robert Kennedy replaced Cohn as Chief Counsel.

The McClellan-Kennedy team made investigating history as it uncovered shocking examples of graft and corruption in labor-management relations. A steady parade of witnesses— Dave Beck, James Hoffa and a galaxy of sordid underworld characters—appeared before the committee. The Kennedy brothers became television "stars." The resultant publicity did much to enhance John F. Kennedy's candidacy for the Presidency.

Although Robert Kennedy's vigorous management of his brother's Presidential campaign gave the impression that he is a strongly partisan Democrat, his administration of the Justice Department has been anything but partisan. He told the writers that he was seeking "the best men, regardless of politics," and noted that one of his principal assistants is Assistant Attorney General Herbert J. Miller of the important Criminal Division, a Republican.

Another Republican who received a job because he impressed Robert Kennedy is Attorney Charles Smith, a former prosecutor from King's County, Washington. In 1957, Mr. Smith was sent to comb over the files of the McClellan Committee for evidence to aid in the prosecution of Dave Beck. Robert Kennedy met, and was impressed by, him. When he became Attorney General, he offered Mr. Smith a job in the Criminal Division despite his GOP politics.

Attorney General Kennedy runs what is best and most picturesquely described in Navy parlance as a "taut ship." Everybody is expected to pitch in and give his utmost. Naturally, with some of the bureaucratic-minded, who are more interested in time-serving than accomplishment, this approach has not been popular. Another of his practices has been received with mixed emotions. This is his habit of popping into Justice Department offices unannounced and saying with a grin: "I'm Bob Kennedy. Who are you? What are you working on?"

These unannounced inspections have revealed both unexpectedly good and unexpectedly bad things about the Justice Department. They revealed, for example, obscure, low-paid attorneys who ordinarily would never see the Attorney General, and who have won praise by working overtime and being the recipient of an unannounced Kennedy visit. On the other hand, at least one attorney has been highly embarrassed by the unannounced visit of Robert Kennedy, who discovered him reading a novel on government time!

Such visits, not entirely popular, have probably given Robert Kennedy a better picture of what is actually going on in the department than any of his predecessors have had for many years. It has also generated a laconic warning among the lethargic at Justice: "Little Brother is watching you!"

The Robert Kennedys live what is considered an "idyllic" family life. Their huge colonial McLean, Virginia, mansion (which incidentally formerly belonged to the present President and First Lady) is one of the historic homes of the Washington area. It is said to have served as the headquarters of General George B. McClellan early in the Civil War.

Mrs. Kennedy, the former Ethel Skakel, is chic, petite and vivacious. She met her energetic husband through his sister Jean (Mrs. Stephen Smith), a college roommate of hers at Manhattanville College. The school, incidentally, was also the alma mater of Robert's mother.

She was considered one of the top-echelon family vote-getters for John Kennedy during the primary and later election campaigns. She was dubbed, in fact, "Miss Perpetual Animation of 1960" by an admiring photographer on the Kennedy campaign trail.

The Kennedys' "idyllic life" is a quiet one. They seldom entertain formally, but almost always have a few guests in for small dinner parties. Most of these guests are not from Washington's elite society. They are more apt to be long-standing friends in the newspaper business.

Charles Bartlett and his wife, who are famous for having been the matchmaking couple who introduced the President to Jacqueline Bouvier, are close friends of the Robert Kennedys. Their four children regularly go out to McLean to play with the large Kennedy brood. Bartlett was once laughingly quoted as saying about his VIP host: "You have to watch Bob. He's always fixing the races so the Kennedy kids will win."

The Attorney General was designated America's "Father of the Year" in 1960. His seven children—Kathleen, Joseph, Robert, David, Mary Courtney, Michael and Mary Kerry— have a private menagerie unrivaled in the area. Among their large collection of pets are three dogs, cats, ducks, rabbits, chickens, ponies and, until recently, a sea lion, who occupied the family swimming pool but who has been given to the Washington Zoo. The aquatic animal, named Sandy, was a sensation as he bobbed about in the water with the children. The Robert Kennedy children have also been the recipients of a great many assorted pets sent to "Uncle Jack." Much of the overflow of pets intended for Caroline Kennedy in the White House wind up at the Robert Kennedy country home where there is more room than in the executive mansion. At Easter, a batch of eggs, which the children excitedly hoped to hatch into baby ducks, was sent over from the White House, the gift of a Presidential friend. It turned out that the eggs were of the hard-boiled variety and proved quite a disappointment to the young Robert Kennedy children.

Mrs. Kennedy comes from a large family, as does her husband. He was one of nine children, and she comes from a family of six brothers and sisters. Her parents were the late Mr. and Mrs. George Skakel of Greenwich, Connecticut, from whom she inherited a substantial fortune. She and Robert Kennedy were married in 1950 while he was still in law school at the University of Virginia.

Even in the Kennedy family, legendary for its competitive spirit, Robert Kennedy's tremendous drive has made itself felt. His father, Joseph P. Kennedy, Sr., once said: "Jack works as hard as any mortal man can. Bobby just goes a little farther."

One of the President's favorite cartoons reportedly deals with the same theme. From *The New Yorker* magazine, it shows Nikita Khrushchev in pajamas, talking with his wife: "Did I have a nightmare! I dreamt we got the first man on the moon and then it turned out to be Bobby Kennedy!"

It is interesting to speculate whether the famous Robert Kennedy drive comes from a psychological need not to be outdone by other members of his famous family. His grandfather, John Fitzgerald, was Mayor of Boston. His father, Joseph Kennedy, Sr., made one of the world's great fortunes. (It has been estimated as high as $400 million.) He also had a distinguished career in government, serving as Ambassador to Great Britain, Chairman of the Securities and Exchange Commission and Chairman of the Maritime Commission.

In boyhood, Robert Kennedy's eldest brother, Joseph P. Kennedy, Jr., was regarded, according to family legend, as the most likely member of the family to succeed, establishing a record of rare brilliance before he was killed in action in World War II. And, of course, the exploits of John Fitzgerald Kennedy are too well known to require elaboration.

The authors, usually hesitant to offer such an opinion, unhesitatingly predict that Robert Kennedy will be one of the country's great Attorney Generals. He has the talent, the ability and, above all, the sheer determination to do so. To fail or to be mediocre would be very un-Kennedy-like. And he is not the man to let the family tradition down.

Deputy Attorney General Byron White

Robert Kennedy's chief assistant is Deputy Attorney General Byron White, 43, of Colorado. Mr. White will be remembered by all sports fans over thirty years of age as one of the great collegiate football players of all time. In 1938, closing his career at Colorado University, he made everybody's All-America team. A brilliant scholar as well as an outstanding athlete, Mr. White was president of the student body, valedictorian of his class, Phi Beta Kappa, and a Rhodes Scholar.

While in London studying at Oxford University, White and future President John Kennedy met and became friends. Their paths crossed again in 1943 when both were serving with the Navy in the Solomons campaign. They met again in 1947 when White was law clerk to Chief Justice Fred Vinson of the United States Supreme Court, and John F. Kennedy was a freshman Congressman from Massachusetts. Mr. White was one of the earliest "Kennedy-for-President" backers.

Solicitor General Archibald Cox

The Solicitor General is the man who argues cases before the Supreme Court. As Solicitor General, Mr. Cox will be the nation's number one courtroom lawyer.

An early Kennedy adviser, Cox, 48, was born in Plainfield, New Jersey. He attended Harvard Law School, and served on the Solicitor General's staff from 1941 to 1943. Mr. Cox was Royall Professor of Law at Harvard Law School prior to accepting appointment as Solicitor General.

Director of the Federal Bureau of Investigation
J. Edgar Hoover

The most famous of all Justice Department personnel is J. Edgar Hoover, legendary chief of the FBI. When President John Kennedy's election was certain, the first federal officials he asked to remain on the job from the Eisenhower Administration were J. Edgar Hoover and Allen Dulles, Director of the super-secret Central Intelligence Agency.

As the man who made the "G-men" an effective law enforcement agency and who directed the FBI's war on such criminals as John Dillinger, Baby Face Nelson, Pretty Boy Floyd and a host of other notorious desperadoes, Mr. Hoover has been a national hero for more than three decades.

Under his leadership, the FBI's crime laboratory has become a scientific bulwark in the war on crime. (Incidentally, for readers who visit Washington, D.C., the free tour of the FBI labs, including many exhibits showing details of the bureau's work, is among Washington's most fascinating sights. Too many visitors miss it, not knowing of its existence.)

J. Edgar Hoover was born New Year's Day, 1895, in Washington, D.C. He graduated from George Washington University College and Law School. In 1917, he entered the Department of Justice and two years later was named Special Assistant to the Attorney General. From 1921 until 1924 he served as Assistant Director of the FBI, when he was named Director. He has held the post ever since.

Assistant Attorney General Herbert J. Miller, Jr. (Criminal Division)

Mr. Miller, 36, a Republican, was born in Minneapolis. He graduated from West High School there and received his undergraduate education at both the University of Minnesota and George Washington University. During World War II he entered the Army as a private and was separated with the rank of captain. He returned to George Washington University and graduated from its Law School in 1949. Until his appointment, he practiced law with a Washington firm.

Assistant Attorney General Ramsey Clark (Lands Division)

Mr. Clark, 34, is the son of United States Supreme Court Justice Tom Clark. A Texan, he served in the Marine Corps, attended the Universities of Texas and Chicago. For ten years, he practiced law in Dallas, then gave up his business to take on the vast job of supervising all litigation relating to federal acquisition, ownership and use of land, including conservation and reclamation programs and civil litigation affecting Indians.

Assistant Attorney General Burke Marshall
(Civil Rights Division)

Mr. Marshall has over-all responsibility for the enforcement of the laws in the general field of civil rights, including laws relating to voting, elections and corrupt practices; illegal deprivations of the rights of citizens; obstruction of justice; sentencing of federal prisoners; and the protection of merchant seamen.

Mr. Marshall, 39, was born in Plainfield, New Jersey. He served in the Army during the Second World War, and attended Yale Law School. From 1952 until his appointment, he was a partner in a law firm which included former Secretary of State Dean Acheson.

Assistant Attorney General William H. Orrick, Jr.
(Civil Division)

Except in very special cases, the Civil Division of the Justice Department handles all non-criminal lawsuits to which the United States is a party. This is a vast responsibility and includes a wide variety of legal actions, ranging from Admiralty suits, claims against the United States, and patents. Mr. Orrick, 45, is a Californian, who attended Yale and the University of California Law School. He served in the Army and practiced law in San Francisco.

Assistant Attorney General Lee Loevinger
(Anti-Trust Division)

The Anti-Trust Division is one of the hottest spots in the whole government. It is responsible for enforcement of the Sherman Anti-Trust Act, the Clayton Act and supplementary laws.

Justice Loevinger graduated from the University of Minnesota Law School, served in the Navy between 1942 and 1945, practiced law in Kansas City, Missouri, served as an attorney with the National Labor Relations Board and the Anti-Trust Division, and practiced law in Minneapolis prior to his appointment to Minnesota's highest court.

Assistant Attorney General Nicholas deB. Katzenbach
(Office of Legal Counsel)

Mr. Katzenbach, 39, is a former law professor at the University of Chicago. He also was on the staff of Yale's Law

School and practiced law in Trenton, New Jersey. He was educated at Princeton and Yale Law School and was a Rhodes Scholar. During World War II he was a captain in the Air Force, was a prisoner of war in Germany, and won numerous decorations.

Assistant Attorney General Louis F. Oberdorfer
(Tax Division)

Head of the Tax Division is a former Washington, D.C., lawyer. Mr. Oberdorfer, a native of Birmingham, Alabama, has a law degree from Yale University. He was at one time the law clerk to Supreme Court Justice Hugo L. Black. He served in the Army Artillery Corps, rising from private to captain, during World War II. He went into private law practice and has specialized in tax law during his legal career before being appointed an Assistant Attorney General.

Commissioner Joseph May Swing
(Immigration and Naturalization Service)

The Immigration and Naturalization Service, under the direction of Commissioner Swing, administers the Immigration and Nationality Act and related laws for the United States Government. This office has four regional offices, thirty-two district offices and more than five-hundred field offices located throughout the United States, principally at ports of entry to this country, where aliens are examined to determine their admissibility under federal laws. Investigations, detentions, deportation and registration matters are also handled by these offices.

General Swing is a graduate of West Point. He retired from the Army in 1954 after a distinguished career. In 1916, he served on the Punitive Expedition in Mexico. In World War I, he served in France, and in World War II, he served in the Pacific theater.

Director of the Federal Bureau of Prisons James V. Bennett

Director Bennett has charge of the twenty-eight federal penal and correctional institutions of the United States. The son of a New York State minister, he received his education at Brown University and has a law degree from George Washington University in Washington, D.C.

He was a cadet aviator in World War I. He has been Director of the Bureau of Prisons since 1937 and was reappointed to that office by President Kennedy.

CHAPTER TWO

Dean Rusk and the State Department

THE OFFICE——Few, if any, would dispute that the Secretary of State is the most important member of the Cabinet. He is the ranking Cabinet member, sits at the President's right hand at Cabinet meetings, and is the President's chief adviser on foreign affairs. So significant have the Secretary of State's duties become—considering the important issues of war or peace, and perhaps even of mankind's survival—that many observers believe that the Secretary of State is, next to the President, the most important official in the nation.

The State Department and Foreign Service of the United States are sometimes called "America's front line troops in time of peace." Their success in performing their task can weigh enormously in creating a peaceful, prosperous world. Failure could spell disaster—for the United States, for the free world, and perhaps for the whole human race.

So complex and interdependent is our modern world that rumblings anywhere in the globe—revolution in Cuba, upheaval in the Congo or Laos, riots in South America, assassinations in the Middle East—immediately have repercussions felt in El Paso or Des Moines.

The horrifying possibilities created by modern science—missile warfare with hydrogen or cobalt bombs—have given an urgency to modern diplomacy that is testing it to the utmost. But the intricacies of foreign affairs, already unbelievably complex, are becoming more so daily.

The expansion of the so-called "nuclear club" (nations capable of producing an atomic bomb) and the rise of the Communist Chinese government are two items in point. The day may shortly come when even a score of petty and irresponsible dictators may possess the means of beginning a holocaust which could obliterate mankind.

This puts staggering responsibilities on the American Secretary of State. What sort of an "army" does the Secretary of State command in his quest for peace?

22

At the present writing, the State Department employs some 23,500 persons. (The actual number varies from time to time, of course.) At the current writing, the United States has diplomatic relations with 98 countries (reduced by two by the severing of diplomatic ties with the Dominican Republic and Cuba). New nations are being created rapidly in Africa, and this number is increasing.

Some 6,500 State Department employees are stationed in Washington. A few more than 700 are in other parts of the United States, and the rest are scattered among the 94 embassies, 4 legations, 4 missions, 68 consulates general, 97 consulates and 21 consular agencies which the nation maintains. The cost of operating the department is currently about $260 million a year.

The State Department is the oldest Executive Department of the government. The first "official" Secretary of State was Thomas Jefferson, but John Jay was the first acting Secretary of State under the Constitution. He had been Secretary for Foreign Affairs under the old Continental system and stayed on until Jefferson, then Minister to France, tidied up his work and returned home to take office on March 22, 1790. On September 15, 1789, by Act of Congress, the State Department acquired its current name. Until then, it had been the Department of Foreign Affairs.

The list of Secretaries of State reads almost like a "Who's Who" of American history. It includes six Presidents— Thomas Jefferson, James Madison, James Monroe, John Quincy Adams, Martin Van Buren and James Buchanan— and many Presidential aspirants, such as Henry Clay, Daniel Webster, John C. Calhoun, James G. Blaine, William Jennings Bryan and Charles Evans Hughes. For many decades, the Secretaryship of State was the steppingstone to the Presidency.

Richard S. Patterson, State Department historian, told the writers that, among diplomatic scholars, John Quincy Adams is generally conceded to have been the most brilliant and successful Secretary of State, and many rank William H. Seward next after Adams. Adams collaborated with President Monroe in formulating the Monroe Doctrine and skillfully maneuvered the Spanish into giving the United States a boundary westward to the Pacific Ocean. Seward successfully conducted the delicate relations of the United States with foreign nations throughout the Civil War, and he subsequently negotiated the treaty with Russia for the cession of Alaska. After Adams and Seward, Historian Patterson says, there is vast disagreement as to who was the third most skillful Secretary of State. Secretaries of State are almost invariably highly controversial. A Secretary who to millions may seem a great statesman may to other millions seem an inept or actually dangerous politician. Other notable Secretaries of State, besides those previously mentioned, include Edward Everett, Lewis Cass, Hamilton Fish, John Hay, Elihu Root, Robert Lansing, Henry L. Stimson, Cordell Hull, George C. Marshall, Dean Acheson and John Foster Dulles.

Cordell Hull served in the office longer than any other man, from March 4, 1933, until November 30, 1944. Secretary Hull won the Nobel Peace Prize and is called by some the "father" of the United Nations for his work in its founding.

Under the Constitution, the making of foreign policy rests with the President. In the press, there is much written about "strong" Presidents "who are their own Secretaries of State" as contrasted with "strong" Secretaries of State and "weak" Presidents. Such talk is misleading and almost meaningless. The Secretary of State and the vast galaxy of specialists in the State Department may *advise,* but, when the chips are down, it is the President who must take the responsibility for all decisions.

(It's interesting to note that while the President receives the advice of any member of the Cabinet he is not bound to follow it unless he so desires. The classic story which illustrates this is that of Abraham Lincoln's Emancipation Proclamation. After reading it to the Cabinet, so the story goes, the seven members of the Cabinet were unanimously against it. [Three new Cabinet members have been added since Lincoln's time.] "That makes seven nos and one aye," Lincoln said with a grin. "The ayes have it.")

On the other hand, it is true that some Presidents keep a closer, day-to-day watch on foreign affairs than others. Recent examples of such "strong" Presidents include Woodrow Wilson, Franklin Roosevelt and undoubtedly President Kennedy.

The Foreign Service——Approximately 9,000 members of the State Department are Foreign Service officers.

Foreign Service posts fall into two broad categories— diplomatic and consular. Chiefs of diplomatic missions, both embassies and legations, are appointed by the President and accredited to the chief of state of the host country. An embassy is headed by an ambassador and a legation by a minister. An embassador is the personal representative of the President, though a minister may also represent the President in negotiations with the foreign government to which he is accredited. Embassies and legations usually are located in the capital city of the host country.

Consular posts are established in various important cities in a country in accordance with need and on authorization granted by the host government. Consular officers are not accredited to the host government and are not authorized to represent the President in negotiations with foreign governments.

Establishment of a consular post in a country does not depend upon the existence of diplomatic relations and does not imply diplomatic recognition. The function of a consular officer is to perform various traditional services such as the issuance of visas and passports, protection of American citizens and property, and assistance to American businessmen, as well as services to American shipping and seamen. He also bears important responsibilities with regard to representation and political and economic reporting. Consular posts in each country with which the United States maintains diplomatic relations are under the supervision of the United States diplomatic mission in that country.

Foreign Service officers and their families are often the unsung heroes of the battle for peace. More than a third of all posts in the Foreign Service are classified as "hardship posts." In such places lack of comfortable and sanitary housing, adequate medical care, modern sanitation, the presence of disease, extremes of heat and cold, civil disturbances, riots, revolution and the like are everyday hazards.

Considering the high personal and professional qualifications required, Foreign Service pay is low and out-of-pocket expenses are high. Official allowances often do not cover obligatory expenses of entertaining, of sending children away to school when local schools are inadequate or nonexistent.

THE MAN——There is one remarkable fact about the selection of soft-spoken, Georgia-born Dean Rusk, 52, as Secretary of State, which deserves more attention than the casual mention it has received in the press.

It is this: Mr. Rusk was chosen entirely for his professional competence, not because of any political power. Most previous Secretaries of State, even great ones, have been men of great political influence. The official transcript of then President-Elect Kennedy's announcement of Secretary Rusk's appointment and his exchange of comments with newspaper reporters lightly passes over what amounts to a revolution in America's methods of choosing Cabinet officers:

REPORTER: (to President-Elect Kennedy) Could you tell us how Dean Rusk came to your attention for this job?

PRESIDENT-ELECT KENNEDY: Well, I have given the matter of the Secretary of State a good deal of thought, and it has been a matter, really, of prime concern since the election. Dean Rusk was, *it seemed to me after a long and careful study of the responsibilities of the office, it seemed to me to be the best man available that the United States could get.*

Q. How long have you known him, sir?

A. I have just come to know him. I met him for the first time this week.

Q. Last week?

A. Last week.

In the opinion of the authors, this illustrates dramatically the changing nature of the Cabinet. Secretary Rusk's selection shows how Cabinet posts have grown to positions of such staggering complexity that political influence must be subordinated to professional know-how.

Even such a great Secretary of State as Cordell Hull, who served under President Franklin D. Roosevelt, was chosen at least in part because of his great influence in the United States Senate and on Capitol Hill generally. There seem to have been times when Under Secretary of State Sumner Welles was more in the President's confidence and was closer to him than was the Secretary.

So recent is the trend toward picking men for their skill and professional standing that, when, in June, 1915, President Woodrow Wilson named State Department Counselor Robert Lansing Secretary of State to succeed the resigned William Jennings Bryan, it was thought an astounding departure from standard practice. Lansing was the foremost international lawyer of his day and a skilled diplomat and negotiator, but he had negligible, if any, real political influence. The appointment was widely applauded as a praiseworthy innovation by the "professor President," Wilson.

So rapidly has the world moved that what in Wilson's day was a remarkable innovation has now become almost routine. Six of the ten members of President Kennedy's Cabinet—Mr.

Rusk, Secretary of the Treasury Douglas Dillon, Secretary of Labor Arthur Goldberg, Secretary of Defense Robert McNamara, Attorney General Robert Kennedy and Postmaster General Edward Day—have never been candidates for any elective public office!

None of the "Big Three" of the Cabinet—Secretary of State Rusk, Secretary of the Treasury Dillon and Secretary of Defense McNamara—are men with substantial political influence. Dillon and McNamara are actually registered Republicans. This dramatically illustrates how professional competence has become a requirement for such important posts.

Mr. Rusk was born on February 9, 1909, in Cherokee County, Georgia. "This obviously makes me a Democrat," he smiles. His father was a postal employee. He went to Boys' High in Atlanta, where he had a brilliant scholastic record. Even then, he was interested in working for world peace. His brother, Parks Rusk, recalled that, in high school debates, "Dean always took the side of the old League of Nations even when it was not popular to do so." He had a preoccupation with international affairs and working for world peace unusual in one so young, his brother says.

Dean Rusk graduated from Davidson College in 1931, got an A.B. degree from the University of North Carolina in 1933. Like many other members of the Kennedy Cabinet, he won a coveted Phi Beta Kappa key, and he was a Rhodes Scholar.

One of the oft-told stories about Secretary Rusk is how, when he was applying for a Rhodes scholarship, he stated on his application that he wished to study at Oxford for the purpose of preparing himself for a career devoted to furthering the cause of world peace.

"But," challenged one of the board examining him, "you've been very active in the cadet corps and an ROTC officer all through you high school and college career. Isn't this a contradiction with a career seeking peace?"

"No," said the young Rusk. "If you'll look at the Great Seal of the United States, you'll find that the eagle holds an olive branch in one talon and a bundle of arrows in the other."

From 1934 to 1940, Secretary Rusk was associate professor of government and Dean of the Faculty at Mills College in Oakland, California. It was at Mills College that the Secretary met his wife, the former Virginia Foisie. She was a student in his international relations class. They were married in 1937.

Rusk's pleasant academic life was disrupted by war. His ROTC background had given him a commission as a captain in the Army Reserve and, in 1940, he was called to active duty and placed in the British Section of Army Intelligence. Later, he was sent to India, where he took part in two vicious jungle campaigns in Burma. He rose to the rank of full colonel, and served as assistant chief of staff for the whole theater. He flew the dangerous "Hump" fourteen times and won the Legion of Merit and the Oak Leaf Cluster.

Returning to Washington, Rusk's government career began in earnest. He held numerous posts in the State Department and the War Department. In 1949, he was appointed Deputy Under Secretary of State, after serving in such posts as Assistant Chief of the Division of International Security Affairs for the State Department; Special Assistant to the Secretary of War (1946-47); Director of United Nations Affairs for the Department of State (1947-49).

In 1950, he took what was nominally a "demotion" to handle a trouble spot—Assistant Secretary of State for Far Eastern Affairs. It was in this post that he played an important role in the American decision to intervene in Korea in 1950 when the Communists invaded South Korea from the north.

The incident was recalled to the authors recently by Pyo Wook Han, former Minister to the United States from the Republic of Korea. (Mr. Han, a noted scholar on Far Eastern affairs, is better known to his wide circle of friends in Washington as "Phil.")

"I was then First Secretary of the Korean Embassy," Mr. Han recalls, "when, about eight-forty-five on the evening of June 24, 1950, I received a call from a friend in the Washington Bureau of the United Press, informing me of the North Korean invasion. I at once called Ambassador Chang [Dr. John M. Chang, present President of Korea] and notified him of what had happened. Then we called the Duty Officer at the State Department. An emergency meeting with Assistant Secretary Dean Rusk was arranged as quickly as possible. Mr. Rusk arrived in evening dress. He'd been called away from a party.

"The meeting lasted about an hour. Later that evening, a second meeting was held which lasted until one o'clock. We had the feeling that Secretary Rusk knew immediately what must be done. The situation must come before the United Nations and the free world must halt the Communist aggression. I believe that Mr. Rusk played an important part in

28

persuading Secretary of State Dean Acheson and President Truman to intervene in Korea."

In March, 1952, Mr. Rusk left the government to become President of the fabulously wealthy Rockefeller Foundation. In that capacity, he directed the spending of over $250 *million* on various charitable and educational projects. One project, presided over by Mr. Rusk, was a study of the office of Secretary of State as an institution. The Rockefeller Brothers Fund Panel, chairmanned by Mr. Rusk, gave a brilliant analysis of why the Secretaryship of State "is almost an impossible office in this country."

The report cites some of the staggering complexities of the President's chief adviser on foreign affairs. There is no better way to comprehend these than in the future Secretary of State's own candid report:

> The public has tended to be mistrustful of the Secretary of State, whatever his political party or whatever the actual policies he has pursued. It has condemned him to spend a disproportionate amount of his time and energies in explaining and justifying his course. It has thus exacted a toll of his vital spirits and of his capacity for objective thinking which can ill be spared. . . .
>
> The Secretary of State has tried to be an administrative officer, to carry on detailed negotiations in different parts of the world, to be a trouble-shooter at various spots of tension, to be the country's representative at innumerable international conferences and its spokesman in the major debates of the United Nations. He is accountable to Congress and to the public through press conferences and constant questioning by congressional committees.
>
> Finally, he is in constant negotiation with powerful domestic agencies in the fields of military power, economic development and information. It has been difficult, in the midst of all this, for the Secretary of State to give to overall policy that continuous thought and attention which diplomatic strategy requires in a world so essentially interrelated, where every problem touches every other.

Like many other members of the Kennedy Cabinet, Dean Rusk took a whopping big salary cut when he became Secretary of State. His salary as head of the Rockefeller Foundation was reportedly $65,000 a year. As Secretary of State, he receives $25,000. Through an odd quirk in the law, several of his subordinates in the State Department receive more than he does. The Ambassadors to Great Britain, the Philippines, France and Russia all receive $27,500 a year.

29

(But, Secretary Rusk reports, an unexpected bonus goes with his job. While at the University of California to make a speech, he remarked that since he became Secretary of State "beautiful young ladies smile at me on the street.")

Attending a Dean Rusk press conference is an exciting event. Television cameras, radio engineers, dozens of photographers and hundreds of correspondents cram into the spacious State Department Auditorium, and, as the Secretary speaks, cameras are flashing almost continually. Topics covered range from the armaments race, to the Congo, Laos, NATO, Cuba and myriad others.

At his first press conference Mr. Rusk casually mentioned a couple of eye-opening facts which indicate something of the huge scope of State Department activities.

"I have been told," he said, "that the cable traffic of the Department of State exceeds every day the combined output of the Associated Press and the United Press International from Washington, D.C." (This amounts to hundreds of thousands of words daily.)

The Secretary mentioned another fact which illustrates the vast scope of America's international relations. Every working day throughout the year, he said rather casually, there are usually from twelve to twenty international meetings going on somewhere in the world at which the United States is represented. To the accompaniment of chuckles from the correspondents, he noted: "Today, I gather, there are only nine. But this is somewhat of an off season."

Secretary Rusk is known as a hard worker. His twelve-hour day usually begins about eight-twenty A.M., when he arrives at his office overlooking the Potomac River, the Lincoln Monument and the Jefferson Memorial. The office is a spacious one with wide windows giving on the handsome view. In one corner of the room stands an old grandfather clock reputed to date from the time of Thomas Jefferson, the first Secretary of State. A television set, symbol of today's world, stands in another corner. On the wall behind the Secretary's wide desk is a relief map of Laos, Cambodia and Vietnam.

Dean Rusk is a tall, rather slender man, who stands a trifle over six feet and weighs about 180 pounds. Balding, he wears dark, horn-rimmed glasses and speaks with a soft, not very noticeable Southern accent.

The Rusks, who like Washington very much, live in the fashionable Spring Valley area of northwest Washington in a handsome but unpretentious two-story home. The family includes David, who is a student at the University of California; Richard, at Wilson High School in Washington; and their subteen daughter, Peggy.

Mrs. Rusk reports that young Peggy is a "gem" around the house, "an excellent cook, beautiful ironer, and good at all the housewifely arts." As for young Richard, he is an expert at woodwork. "Woodworking is his favorite hobby," Mrs. Rusk states, citing the fact that he paneled an entire room in the basement of their home in Scarsdale. She adds, "It's a shame he had to leave all his work in that room behind him."

Their Scarsdale neighbors hated to see the family go, too. One friend said, "I hated to see us lose the ablest chairman of the Scarsdale PTA." Rusk reportedly said on that: "I did it by coaching the youngsters and by putting the fathers to work."

What sort of a man *is* Dean Rusk?

In the opinion of the writers, the most significant clues to his thinking may well be contained in remarks before policy-making officials of the State Department. Almost entirely unnoticed and unpublicized, Secretary Rusk's candid remarks to top brass on "what foreign policy is all about" give something of the flavor of the man himself—and a brilliant analysis of America's role in foreign affairs.

"Older political forms have disintegrated," the Secretary of State declared solemnly. "New international forms are coming into being. We are experiencing enormous pressures to achieve economic and social improvement in all parts of the world, as masses of people who have largely been isolated from currents of world opinion, knowledge and information are coming to realize that their miseries are not a part of an ordained environment about which nothing can be done."

Secretary Rusk then outlined his views on the necessity for a "leadership of change."

"We could be passive in relation to these changes and take our chances . . . were we to be passive, we could not expect the institutions of freedom to survive," he said. "We could undertake an active defense of the *status quo*. My own guess is that, were we to do that, we would be fighting a losing battle. We can, on the other hand, attempt to take a certain leadership in change itself; certainly the world is not as we should like to see it and the world is not as peoples elsewhere find tolerable. . . . What we in the United States do or do not do will make a very large difference in what happens in the rest of the world.

"We in this department must think about foreign policy in its total context. We cannot regard foreign policy as something left over after defense policy or trade policy or fiscal policy has been extracted. Foreign policy is the total involvement of the American people with peoples and governments abroad. . . .

"It is the concern of the Department of State that the American people are safe and secure—defense is not a monopoly concern of the Department of Defense. It also is the concern of the Department of State that our trading relationships with the rest of the world are vigorous, profitable and active—this is not just a passing interest or a matter of concern only to the Department of Commerce. . . .

"I would hope that we could pay attention to little things. While observing the operations of our government in various parts of the world, I have felt that in many situations where our policies were good we have tended to ignore minor problems which spoiled our main effort.

"To cite only a few examples:

"The wrong man in the wrong position, perhaps even in a junior position abroad, can be a source of great harm to our policy; the attitudes of a United Nations delegate who experiences difficulty in finding adequate housing in New York City, or of a foreign diplomat in similar circumstances in our Capital, can easily be directed against the United States and all it stands for. . . .

"The processes of government have sometimes been described as a struggle for power among those holding public office. I am convinced that this is true only in a certain formal and bureaucratic sense, having to do with appropriations, job descriptions, trappings of prestige, water bottles and things of that sort. There is another struggle of far more consequence, the effort to diffuse or avoid responsibility. Power gravitates to those who are willing to make decisions and live with the results, simply because there are so many who readily yield to the intrepid few who take their duties seriously."

Ambassador to the United Nations Adlai E. Stevenson

Despite attacks upon it from some quarters, the overwhelming majority of Americans are firmly convinced that the United Nations offers the last, best hope for peace. The thing that puzzles most Americans is how they can support the UN, and play a role in helping its work.

In preparing this book, the authors wrote to Ambassador Stevenson, asking him to comment on what he most hopes to accomplish as Ambassador to the United Nations and how the average citizen can help support the UN's work. As usual, Mr. Stevenson's answers are a masterpiece of clarity and wisdom. We might begin this profile by setting them forth verbatim. The questions are from the writers. The answers are Ambassador Stevenson's:

What is the stake of the average U. S. citizen in the UN?

AMBASSADOR STEVENSON: "The stake is increasingly one of survival. If nations cannot learn to live together, how much less is the chance for individuals?

But let us look at this situation in perspective: In the second half of this 20th Century we are living through an historical experience which, in all the annals of man, has proven desperately difficult. This experience is the disintegration of one pattern of imperial power and the establishment of new, political relationships and power centers in its place.

Times of imperial collapse are always times of trouble. Today, in fifteen short years, we have seen the dominion which Western Europe exercised over most of Asia and Africa all but vanish. All Asia has emerged from colonial or semi-colonial control. Africa is in the violent throes of the same process.

That such periods of change should be accompanied by ferment and turbulence which we find every day reflected back to us through the UN should be neither surprising nor new.

What is both surprising and new is that the UN is trying to do something about these risks by confronting the old fatalities of collapsing empires with wholly new approaches to the dilemmas of our time.

It is a matter of exhilaration to me that here in America— in the newest of continents and in the midst of perhaps the most far reaching experiment in free, unimperial government —a new start should be underway in the management of human affairs, a new experiment to defeat the set, historical deadlocks of the past.

This, I think, is the profound, historical significance of what is being attempted at the UN. This, I believe, is what is at stake for all our citizens."

What can the average U. S. citizen do to support the work of the UN?

33

AMBASSADOR STEVENSON: "In general I would say to our people, support the UN with your sympathetic attention, your best suggestions and your prayers.

More specifically I would ask that you become more informed of UN activities and programs by following its debates in the newspapers, on radio and TV. Develop closer links with the UN through a variety of non-governmental organizations, such as the American Association for the UN (AAUN) and various foreign policy groups, which publicize its affairs. Make an effort to meet and entertain members of the visiting delegations that tour the U.S. Send your questions or ideas to our U. S. Mission at 799 United Nations Plaza, New York 17, New York, to the UN Office of Public Information at the UN, or to the State Department in Washington, D. C. Finally, visit the UN—preferably with your children—at its headquarters at the earliest opportunity.

If each of you follow through on a few of these suggestions the net result, in terms of support and understanding, will be very sizeable indeed."

What do you most hope to accomplish from your work at the UN?

AMBASSADOR STEVENSON: "I would like to enlarge the areas of peace in the world and to have the satisfaction of feeling that the foundations of international law and order are secure.

It has been said of the UN that 'Since wars begin in the minds of men, it is in the minds of men that the defenses of peace must be constructed.' This ideal recognizes that the UN is a sensitive measure of the tremors which shake the community of nations—tremors which have built up to dangerous levels. But the tremors are man-made, and man can still them. I would hope, therefore, for a wider appreciation among the U. S. public of the increasing role which the UN can play as 'a center for harmonizing the actions of nations.'

Although we find ourselves on the threshold of a nuclear age, with energies that will carry us through the far reaches of outer space, we still share the common yearning of all men, as expressed in the Charter, to achieve freedom from war, poverty, disease, ignorance and oppression. This is what binds us together on earth.

Our security and salvation lie in the ability of nations and governments to see through clouds of conflict and discern the truth about our common interests—and then, boldly and in

34

concert, to act. Let us pray that the record of history will be in our favor."

The enormity of the responsibility Ambassador Stevenson holds as the United States Representative to the United Nations can perhaps best be understood by the realization that in the 1960's the survival of that body may well be decided. With its survival rests the "hope of international amity in honor and freedom" of the world.

Adlai Stevenson is uniquely qualified for the post he holds. He enjoys a rare position of respect and admiration in the world community. When he held his first press conference in New York City with the United Nations Press Corps on January 27, 1961, one of the seasoned reporters in asking a pertinent question of Ambassador Stevenson said, "Perhaps you do not know that many newsmen here are still 'all the way with Adlai.' "

CBS commentator and columnist Eric Sevareid said of him at the time of his appointment: "Stevenson is more than an intellect in operation; he is a kind of presence on stage. He will be more *persona grata* on this stage than any performer we could send. There is a culture of the heart as well as that of the head. Stevenson, thank God, is at home and at ease in both."

When President Kennedy offered Stevenson the appointment to the Ambassadorship to the United Nations, it was the first time he announced a specific appointment proposal without being certain in advance that it would be accepted. The President said that as Mr. Stevenson would fill the role it would become "one of three of four most important jobs in the entire administration." He also said it would have a role in top-level policy-making and assume Cabinet rank.

Stevenson played a major part in the development and planning of the United Nations. He went to the UN Conference at San Francisco in 1945 as a press officer, to London as the key man in the American delegation to the Preparatory Commission. Later he was a delegate to the United Nations General Assembly.

In discussing his return to the United Nations, Ambassador Stevenson said:

"The United Nations is now an organization of ninety-nine member states—double its size when I last served here. We cannot afford to neglect the opportunities which our membership gives us, nor do we intend to do so. We look to the

United Nations not as an arena in which to fight the cold war but, rather, as an instrument which can help us to end it and to liberate man from the scourges of war, poverty, disease, ignorance and oppression. We are not seeking here military alliances; we shall not try to impose our system or philosophy on others. We seek only that they should make good their national independence and advance the well-being of their people."

Adlai Ewing Stevenson was born February 5, 1900, in Los Angeles, California. His family moved to Bloomington, Illinois, when he was a young boy. He was named for his famous grandfather, the Adlai Stevenson who was Vice President of the United States under Grover Cleveland. Another famous ancestor, his great-grandfather, Jesse Fell, was an Illinois pioneer and close friend of Abraham Lincoln. His grandmother, Letitia Green Stevenson, was the founder of the National Congress of Parents and Teachers and one of the co-founders of the Daughters of the American Revolution.

After public school, the young Stevenson went to the elite Choate prep school in Connecticut and then on to Princeton, where he was editor of the college daily newspaper and active in student activities. He also served briefly as an apprentice seaman in the Navy in 1918, which delayed his graduation from Princeton until 1922. He studied law at Harvard Law School but took his law degree from Northwestern University Law School in Chicago.

After college, Stevenson worked on the Bloomington *Pantagraph,* the family-owned newspaper, and later traveled extensively through Europe and Russia as a foreign correspondent. He entered the practice of law in 1927 in the firm of Cutting, Moore & Sidley in Chicago and married in 1928. His wife, from whom he was divorced in 1949, was the former Ellen Borden of the socially prominent Chicago family. They have three sons, Adlai III, Borden and Fell, and two grandchildren, the daughter and son of Adlai III and his wife, Nancy Anderson Stevenson.

Stevenson's actual government service career began in 1933 as a Special Assistant in the Department of Agriculture. He resumed the practice of law in 1935 in Chicago until World War II. From 1941 through 1944, he was an Assistant to Secretary of the Navy Frank Knox, a fellow Chicagoan and newspaperman. Here his major responsibilities included mediating labor-management disputes.

In 1943 Stevenson was appointed Chief of the Economic

Mission to Italy, where he worked out basic formulae for postwar planning for defeated countries—considered by many as one of the major efforts in saving Italy from Communism. The next year he was a member of the War Department Mission to Europe, and in 1945 was appointed an Assistant to Secretary of State James Byrnes, and from there went to help form up the United Nations Charter.

The legend of Stevenson as the most articulate and eloquent candidate in the land running for public office began in Illinois in 1948 when he ran for Governor of the state, teaming up with Paul Douglas, who ran for the Senate that same year. In the election, Stevenson received more votes than ever before cast in Illinois, a plurality of 572,000.

An incidental result of the talent hunt of the New Frontier was the disbanding of Adlai Stevenson's law firm of Stevenson, Rifkind and Wirtz. So many members were taken from the law firm that there was nobody left to carry on! In typical fashion, Mr. Stevenson quipped: "I'm sorry I have but one law firm to give for my country."

Incidentally, at the United Nations, Mr. Stevenson prefers to be called "Governor" rather than "Ambassador." There are so many ambassadors, he explained, that it's hard to tell which one is spoken to—he is the only "Governor."

Ambassador Stevenson has undertaken a remarkable program of personal meetings with the hundreds of delegates to the United Nations and has already met every one of them.

His appearances before the UN provide a world-wide showcase for his eloquence. A brilliant sample of this eloquence was demonstrated by Mr. Stevenson in assuming office, when he said:

"The United States cherishes free institutions and is committed to the growth of law across national and cultural frontiers. We believe our goals and interests are shared with the masses of people throughout the world. We will not shrink from the burdens of our membership in this organization. The United States will not always have its way, we know, but I hope we will always have a decent respect for the opinions of others and will act reasonably in settling disputes, reducing armaments, achieving normal relations, even with those with whom we disagree."

Ambassador Stevenson added a sobering note about the propaganda attacks upon the UN and their destructive effect upon the possibilities for world peace:

"I believe that there has been too great a tendency to use

the forum of the United Nations for narrow propaganda purposes. But the hour is too late, the times too dangerous, for name-calling and rhetorical violence. I believe that the world would benefit from a moratorium on propaganda and abuse and by a return in this great parliament to the courtesy and dignity of traditional diplomatic usage."

Under Secretary of State Chester Bowles

So important have foreign affairs become to the United States that a strong argument could be made that Under Secretary Chester Bowles holds the third most responsible post in the government—behind only President Kennedy and Secretary of State Rusk.

Certainly, Mr. Bowles enjoys a prestige and status that no Under Secretary has enjoyed since the days of Sumner Welles.

The authors interviewed Mr. Bowles in his lush, thick-carpeted offices on the top, seventh, floor of the lavish State Department Building. ("These offices are far too lavish," Mr. Bowles said frankly, reading our taxpayers' minds, "and if I had anything to do with them, they wouldn't be anything like this. But they were here before I came.")

Chester Bowles is a man of delightful personality, ready wit and frank speech. A whole book could be (and several excellent books have been) written about his adventures in politics, diplomacy and as the most legendary advertising man of them all.

Chester Bowles was born in Springfield, Massachusetts, where his great grandfather, Samuel Bowles, had founded and edited the Springfield *Republican*. He attended Yale University and graduated in 1924.

"I always had a strong bent toward government service at a time when few of my classmates did," he told the writers. "Government wasn't popular among college students in those days. Then they thought of going into business, not into government. I think one of the best changes that has been made in the intervening years is that today many of the best college students aspire to a career in government. Shortly after I graduated from Yale, I was offered the possibility of going to China as a young Vice Consul. But my father suddenly became gravely ill and my Foreign Service plans had to be postponed. Due to his lingering illness, the whole thing finally petered out."

Instead, Chester Bowles teamed up with William Benton to form the advertising agency of Benton and Bowles. The stock market crash, the depression, and extremely unfavorable business conditions did not hinder the spectacular growth of the agency into one of the giants of the industry. Perhaps never in the history of American advertising has the record of Benton and Bowles been matched. Chester Bowles was Chairman of the Board of Directors.

"When I started, I determined to stay in the advertising business only five years," Under Secretary Bowles told us. "But it was very difficult to pull out. I finally stayed until I was thirty-nine years old. Then I knew it was time to quit."

Under Secretary Bowles has long since sold out his interest in Benton and Bowles, and from that sale he has been able to devote his life to his real interest—public service.

"The amounts of money I am supposed to have made in advertising have been greatly exaggerated," Mr. Bowles remarked offhandedly to the writers.

When asked if his spectacular advertising career had taught him skills which would be helpful to him in "selling" American ideas and ideals abroad, Chester Bowles thought seriously for a moment. "No," he said, shaking his head. "Advertising is superficial. And in foreign affairs, particularly, we must learn to resist the kind of short-cut thinking prevalent in advertising. Some people seem to think that all we need to do is spend more money on propaganda. But what we need most are good policies. If we have good policies, the other countries of the world will find out about them. Efforts like the Voice of America are important, of course. But the basic thing is to have good policies."

After leaving advertising, Bowles became active in Democratic politics, and, in 1940, was a Connecticut delegate to the historic Democratic National Convention which nominated Franklin Roosevelt for an unprecedented third term.

When World War II erupted, Chester Bowles tried to get into the Navy. "But they rejected me because I have a bad ear," he told the writers.

Instead, he went into the Office of Price Administration in his home State of Connecticut. Bowles did such a good job that, at the request of President Roosevelt, he came to Washington as General Manager of the Office of Price Administration. Shortly thereafter, he was named Director of the wartime rationing and price control agency. He served on the War Production Board and shortly afterward headed the Economic Stabilization Agency.

Chester Bowles debunked the prevalent idea that this post

was a political liability. "There was a lot of talk about it being an unpopular job," he told the writers. "But it really wasn't. In the campaign of 1944, the OPA wasn't even an issue. It would have been if the opposition could have gotten any important political mileage out of it. And when I ran for Governor of Connecticut in 1948, having been OPA Director was a strong political asset."

Mr. Bowles recalled an amusing anecdote about his gubernatorial campaign of 1948. "I was away from home a lot, and I promised the children that, if I *didn't* win, the whole family would go on a lengthy trip to the West Indies. If I won, of course, I'd have to go to work right away getting ready for my administration as Governor. It's interesting the effect that being in public life has on children. We're convinced that they've gained, rather than lost. We've tried to involve them, to teach them what lessons there are to be learned.

"When they were young, we taught them that, if you are in politics, you've got to expect to be defeated sometimes, And 1948 looked like one of those years," Mr. Bowles smiled. "The newspapers predicted a Republican victory, and everyone was certain—frankly, including me—that I couldn't win. The children got more and more excited about that proposed West Indies trip.

"All they would have to do, their mother and I told them, was a certain amount of studying each day. Outside of that, we could all just be together and loaf in the sun. I really think they were terribly disappointed when I won." Mr. Bowles, a man with an infectious laugh, chuckled at the recollection.

Under Secretary of State Bowles has thus had extensive experience in government on three levels: state, national and international.

"My experiences as Governor were among the most fascinating of my life," he said. "I ran for the office because of a deep conviction that there is a tremendous need for responsible government on the local level. There is a need to decentralize government. Unfortunately, in general, state governments have not fulfilled their true role, in my opinion. Part of this is doubtless due to the too-rigid and out-of-date constitutions of most of our states.

"Many states are dominated by rural areas which are not responsive to the needs of our cities. The failure of many state governments has led to an irresistible demand for the federal government to step in and do the things the state

40

governments are failing to do. We see mayors of our large cities by-passing the states and appealing directly to Washington for the help they need."

Bowles' two-year term as Governor of Connecticut was a memorable one, marked by many notable reforms. "It was very difficult," he said smilingly. "There are an astonishing number of persons with a vested interest in bad government."

Mr. Bowles failed for re-election. "It was the greatest disappointment of my life," he told the writers candidly.

What began as a crushing disappointment, however, was quickly turned into the greatest triumph of his career. Bowles' primary interest had always been in the international field. He was a delegate to the first United Nations Educational, Scientific and Cultural Organization in Paris in 1946. In 1947, he was named a special consultant to UN Secretary General Trygve Lie. In 1951, President Truman appointed him Ambassador to India, thereupon initiating one of the brightest periods of the United States' relations with that vastly important Asian nation.

It is safe to say that never before—and perhaps never since —has the United States had so popular an ambassador who so caught the imagination and enthusiasm of the Indian people and leaders. Chester Bowles refused to shut himself and his family up inside the ornate palace which is the American Embassy in New Delhi, seeing only the diplomatic set, meeting the same old faces over and over again in the usual round of parties that often passes for diplomacy abroad.

He and his family moved into a modest house in an Indian residential area; the three Bowles children went to Indian schools; the whole family worked hard at learning Hindi. Instead of riding to work in a sleek, black limousine, Ambassador Bowles often pedaled a bicycle down New Delhi's teeming streets, pausing to stop, speak and become acquainted with the Indian people. As Ambassador, Bowles formed many close and lasting friendships with Indian leaders. Upon his return, he wrote a bestselling book, *Ambassador's Report*, a fascinating account of his experiences.

Mr. Bowles retains an interesting memento of his triumphs as Ambassador to India. The writers noticed that he wore a most unusual tie clip, adorned by striking Oriental figures.

The Under Secretary smiled when we asked him about it. "It was a gift," he explained. "The figures are my name in Hindi."

41

During 1953-58, Chester Bowles was out of public office. His time was mainly spent writing and lecturing. He wrote many articles for leading magazines, and produced five best-selling books: *The New Dimensions of Peace; American Politics in a Revolutionary World; Africa's Challenge to America; Ideas, People and Peace;* and *The Coming Political Breakthrough.* In 1957, he toured Yugoslavia, Poland and Russia, and secured a memorable interview with Nikita Khrushchev.

Under Secretary Bowles paused for a moment to talk writing shop with the authors. "Writing has always come hard for me," he said modestly, ignoring the outstanding success he has enjoyed as an author. "It goes slow. My last book went through thirteen drafts before I was satisfied with it."

In 1958, to the surprise of many, at the urging of Connecticut Democratic party officials, Bowles accepted what seemed a comparatively minor and quite unpromising assignment— the Democratic nomination to Congress from Connecticut's Second District. This looked unpromising on two counts: (1) it was rock-ribbed Republican territory, and (2) the office hardly seemed worthy of Bowles' talents. But party leaders were convinced that the ticket would be stronger with Bowles' name on the ballot and he agreed to make the uphill fight. Somewhat surprisingly, he won. He was appointed to the Foreign Affairs Committee, unusual for a first-term Congressman.

Under Secretary Bowles spoke warmly, however, of his congressional service. "It was immensely worth while," he declared with the enthusiasm which typifies him. "It opened a whole new world to me. It gave me an entirely new point of view."

In 1959, Chester Bowles joined the Kennedy-for-President camp. He became a foreign affairs adviser to the Massachusetts Senator, and was a familiar figure to millions who followed the 1960 Democratic National Convention on television. He was the chairman of the party's Platform Committee and led the fight for its adoption.

As Under Secretary of State, Chester Bowles has laid great stress on the value of American ambassadors' knowing the language of the country to which they are assigned. For generations, American ambassadors have, on the whole, been among the poorest-prepared of any in the world. This seems to stem from the long-standing American practice of granting ambassadorships as political "plums" to heavy campaign

42

contributors and party faithful. (Both parties have been guilty of this, and it is not until very recent times that the practice has—fortunately—begun to change.)

"We have been urging a new approach among our ambassadors," Mr. Bowles told the writers. "We're telling them: 'Get out of the cities. Get into the rural areas. Meet the people. Meet schoolteachers, the leaders of the peasant groups. Know and speak the language.'

"An important thing for Americans to remember in thinking about world affairs," Mr. Bowles went on, "is that the Communists didn't create the ferment that's going on among the underdeveloped peoples of the world. They *are* trying to take advantage of it, of course."

The Under Secretary of State had some profound things to say on the subject of aid to underdeveloped countries.

"Foreign aid is not just to help them produce more *things*," Mr. Bowles said, "though that is partly true, of course. It's not just a matter of *what* is produced, either. It's a matter of justice. The questions we must ask are: 'What's happening to the *people?* Do they have a sense of participating and belonging?' What happens to the people of the country and how they are affected by our aid is the most important thing."

Mr. Bowles pointed to two familiar foreign aid projects— the dam and the school. "If the dam benefits only the great landlords and doesn't help the peasants, it's hardly worth while. A school, on the other hand, really helps. In foreign aid, we must be sure that what we are doing really gets down to the people's level. We must have a better sense of justice."

In 1934, the Under Secretary of State was married to the former Dorothy Stebbins. There are five Bowles children: Barbara, Chester, Jr., Cynthia, Sarah and Samuel.

Mrs. Bowles, a Washington favorite, has been very helpful to her husband's diplomatic career. A typical instance of this was a recent State Department tea where Mrs. Bowles welcomed visiting churchwomen from all over the world. She spoke to the visitors in six languages: English, Hindi (an Indian dialect), French, Spanish, Tagalog (the language of the Philippine Islands) and Serbo-Croatian.

Under Secretary of State George W. Ball (Economic Affairs)

Washington attorney George W. Ball succeeded C. Douglas Dillon, now Secretary of the Treasury, in the post he now holds. (Under the Eisenhower Administration, Mr. Dillon

43

held the combined offices of Under Secretary of State and the same post for Economic Affairs.) Mr. Ball attended Northwestern University, from which he holds the A.B. and J.D. degrees.

In 1942, he was appointed Associate General Counsel of the Lend-Lease Administration. In 1944-45 he was Director of the United States Strategic Bombing Survey, based in London. From 1946 until he assumed his present post, Mr. Ball was a member of the law firm of Cleary, Gottlieb, Steen and Ball, with offices in New York, Washington, Paris and Brussels.

He is married to the former Ruth Murdoch. They have two sons, John, a student at the American University at Beirut, and Douglas, a student at Wooster College in Ohio.

Ambassador-at-Large W. Averell Harriman

When Averell Harriman was being examined by the Senate Foreign Relations Committee, Chairman J. William Fulbright of Arkansas asked him a tongue-in-cheek question.

"Mr. Harriman," asked Senator Fulbright, "do you know what your salary will be in your new post?"

Averell Harriman, who is used to good-natured hazing by his colleagues in government because of his stupendous fortune, grinned and confessed that he had "no idea" of what his pay was to be.

"I take it that it is not a matter of the highest concern to you," Senator Fulbright said with a smile.

Mr. Harriman possesses both a tremendous fortune and a tremendous record of public service. For thirty years, he has been in and out of government, tackling with rare determination some of the most difficult and delicate assignments.

As the "roving ambassador" of the Kennedy Administration, he will perform a task he undertook very successfully for two other Presidents—trouble-shooting in spots of world crisis. He often acted as the special envoy of Presidents Franklin D. Roosevelt and Harry S. Truman.

Mr. Harriman was born in New York City in 1891. He graduated from Groton and Yale, and then went into business as Vice President in charge of Purchasing and Supplies for the family-owned Union Pacific Railroad. Later, he became a Director of the Illinois Central Railroad, and in the 1920's organized his own banking firm, which has since consolidated with a private banking firm as Brown Brothers, Harriman & Company.

44

In 1933, President Franklin D. Roosevelt appointed Averell Harriman to the Business Advisory Council for the Department of Commerce. He was also named as Administrator of the National Recovery Program during these early depression years. During the early months of 1941, he served with the Office of Production Management and later in that year as President Roosevelt's Special Representative with the rank of Minister to Great Britain.

From 1943 to 1946, Mr. Harriman served in the critically important ambassadorship to the Soviet Union, where he learned much about the Russian people and government during World War II and its early aftermath. He later served briefly as Ambassador to Great Britain, and as Secretary of Commerce under President Truman.

Throughout the late 1940's and early 1950's, he served in a variety of special posts for President Truman, ending with the Directorship of the Mutual Security Administration. He was elected Governor of New York in 1954 and served through 1958.

He has since traveled widely to most of the trouble-spot areas of the world, especially the Far East, Russia and Africa.

As Ambassador-at-Large, Mr. Harriman is available to the President and the Secretary of State for important special missions requiring a spokesman of international stature and prestige who has the full confidence of his chief plus an intimate knowledge of all aspects of our foreign policy.

"The very nature of the appointment requires flexibility," says an aide, who reports that routine assignments or usual channels of consultation between our government and other world leaders will not be changed or interrupted by Ambassador Harriman's special and unique position. When not on special mission, Ambassador Harriman works closely with the President's policy advisers in Washington and most particularly with the Secretary of State.

Mr. Harriman and his second wife, the former Marie Norton Whitney, have taken a house in Georgetown for the duration of his term of office in the Kennedy Administration. The house, a handsome rented mansion on the historic P Street section of the city, already contains many of the couple's most famous French paintings. Many others are on view in the National Gallery of Art and elsewhere.

Other State Department officials of unusual interest include:

Assistant Secretary of State Harlan Cleveland
(International Organization Affairs)

A New Yorker, Mr. Cleveland graduated from Princeton and was a Rhodes Scholar. His government service has been with the Department of Agriculture, the Board of Economic Warfare, and as Executive Director of the Economic Section of the Allied Control Commission in Rome. He has also been with the Economic Co-operation Administration and has represented the United States at many international conferences. He served as Executive Editor of the *Reporter* Magazine and was Dean of the School of Public Administration at Syracuse University.

Assistant Secretary of State Brooks Hays
(Congressional Relations)

Mr. Hays had a distinguished career in the U. S. House of Representatives from 1943 through 1959, serving as a member of the Foreign Affairs Committee his last three terms. He was a representative of the United States to the tenth session of the UN General Assembly in 1955. He left a post as a member of the Board of Directors of the TVA to accept his present post.

Assistant Secretary of State G. Mennen Williams
(African Affairs)

Mr. Williams is a former six-term Governor of Michigan. His was the first new appointment announced by President Kennedy, and his appointment was widely heralded as indicative of increased interest in Africa. He served in the Navy and was Deputy OPA Director of Michigan before being elected Governor. He attended Princeton and Michigan Law School.

CHAPTER THREE

Robert McNamara and the Defense Department

THE OFFICE——The Department of Defense is relatively new as government departments go. It came into being with the enactment of the National Security Act of July 26, 1947. The first Secretary of Defense, James Forrestal, took office on the following September 17. Its problems, its scope and its responsibilities are awesome.

In fact, someone once said, "It is the most complex and difficult post in the government." They may have been right. The decisions made by the Secretary of Defense affect the very survival of the United States and its 180,000,000 inhabitants.

The Secretary of Defense wears many hats. He directs the world's largest number of employees, both civilian and military, in the world's largest office building. From his handsome third-floor office in the oddly designed, five-sided Pentagon (which covers thirty-four acres of land), the Defense Department chief must insure "by timely and effective military action" the security of the country and all its possessions and "areas vital to its interest."

Within the 3,5000,000 employees of the department are included the right arms of the Secretary—the Joint Chiefs of Staff, the military departments of the Secretaries of Navy, Army and Air Force—and, of course, all the personnel of the Army, Navy and Air Force. The Secretary relies on these men to fulfill his function as the chief military adviser to the President of the United States. On the Defense establishment the people of the United States—and the free peoples of the world—rely for military strength to insure the safety of the country and deter aggression.

The department's activities range, in the words of one observer, "from the formation of nuclear war strategy to the care and feeding of servicemen's infants."

The Secretary of Defense is concerned in the recruiting, training, equipping and transportation of military personnel, of whom about 500,000 are overseas. He also "feeds, clothes, houses, pays, hospitalizes, insures and buries" them at various stages of jurisdiction of the Department of Defense over its military personnel and their dependents.

The complexity and diversification of the Defense Department is staggering. Unlike the Departments of Agriculture or Labor, where specific functions and duties are concerned with a relatively narrow field, Defense is all-encompassing. Its physical assets are estimated in excess of $150 *billion*. Its budget is equally staggering—some $45 billion annually— more than half of the national budget. This adds up to more than $500 for every man, woman and child in the United States every year.

The problem of military preparedness is a series of vexing

47

dilemmas. For example, "strategic targeting" is a complex and many-sided problem. Upon its solution may rest the fate of the world. Should the "counterforce policy" prevail? In this, an inventory of nuclear weapons is stockpiled so large that in any attack or catastrophe enough would be left over to attack and destroy the enemy's military forces. Should the so-called "finite policy" be pursued? This policy provides only that number of nuclear weapons which is required to survive a first strike and destroy the enemy's major population centers.

As this book is written, the United States reportedly has, in addition to its Polaris submarines, only nine ICBM (Atlas) missiles, with three launching pads at Vandenburg Air Force Base in California and six such operational installations at Warren Air Force Base near Cheyenne, Wyoming.

Some estimates indicate that Russia has more than fifty operational ICBM's. Furthermore, the Russian missiles carry a warhead, it is believed, which is larger than the United States Atlas carries.

Against these Russian missiles, the diversified character of U. S. retaliatory forces places an enormous defensive burden on potential enemies. There are, for example, the jet bombers in the Strategic Air Command. Each has hydrogen bombs as its "payload." Twenty-two warships have been converted or newly constructed for employment of guided missiles, and forty-five others have been authorized, with more to come.

"A new age in ship propulsion" has been launched as well. Forty-nine nuclear-propelled warships, which include a carrier and a cruiser, have been authorized, and Polaris submarines now in commission form the heart of a fleet of atomic subs.

A second generation of solid-fuel ICBM's, the Minutemen, are currently being developed to be ready in mid-'62. These latter missiles are designed for launching from mobile, as well as fixed, positions. The Kennedy Administration is pushing the expansion program of nuclear submarines, armed with nuclear missiles, rapidly.

Not long after assuming command at the Pentagon, Mc-Namara spoke before the House Armed Services Committee to convince the group to authorize the largest single money bill ever introduced to the Congress—some $11.9 billion in defense measures for new missiles, warplanes and ships, but cutting back on B-70 bomber production and an atomic plane project proposed by the previous administration. "In reevaluating our general war position," he said, "our major concern was to reduce our dependence on deterrent forces which are highly vulnerable to ballistic missile attack or which rely for their survival on a hair-trigger response to the first indications of such an attack.

"We sought to place greater emphasis on the second approach—the kind of forces which could ride out a massive nuclear attack and which could be applied with deliberation and always under the complete control of the constituted authority."

The Defense Department has, too, an additional weapon— a strong continental defense system which has been established with Canada. It includes the controversial "DEW line," which is a defensive construction stretching literally across the top of the world from the Pacific to the Atlantic on the northern edges of the North American Continent.

All of this is but a small part of the job of the Secretary of Defense—a job fraught with frustrations, not the least of which is a smothering aura of what one highly knowledgeable observer of military affairs calls "Pentagon dynamics."

These dynamics involve many special interests—those of the Army, the Navy and the Air Force, politics, industry and labor unions. These forces can reach congressional leaders with their special "projects," stalling and waylaying the decisions of the Secretary of Defense in getting the job done. It is a job for a strong man.

THE MAN——Meeting and interviewing Robert McNamara gave the writers their biggest surprise encountered in preparing this book. Mr. McNamara's pictures do not do him justice. They usually tend to show him looking somewhat grim. And since most business tycoons who come to Washington via Detroit or other big business centers tend to be remote, aloof, humorless men, highly conscious of their own dignity, the writers were prepared to encounter a man of this mold in interviewing Secretary McNamara.

We were quite startled to discover that Secretary McNamara is a warm and really delightful man. He smiles and laughs easily. There is an easy informality about the way he introduces himself—"Hello, I'm Bob McNamara"—that puts the visitor instantly at ease, despite the impressiveness of the Secretary's office in the vast labyrinth of the Pentagon.

Perhaps never before in history has a man paid such a high

price for the privilege of serving his country in a difficult and thankless job as Mr. McNamara has paid to become Secretary of Defense.

He took a 95 per cent reduction in salary (from $475,000 a year plus bonuses as President of the Ford Motor Company to $25,000 a year as Secretary of Defense). And this was only the beginning of the financial sacrifice Mr. McNamara was required to make to take the third-ranking post in the Kennedy Cabinet.

As President of Ford, the quiet, dark-haired, youngish man of 44 had options on 30,000 shares of Ford Motor Company stock, which gave him the privilege of buying stock at prices far below those which prevail upon the New York Stock Exchange. To avoid the problem of "conflict of interest" (since the Ford Motor Company does business with the Department of Defense), McNamara voluntarily gave up his stock options.

At the time President-Elect Kennedy announced his appointment, McNamara estimated that the loss of these options would cost him between three and four million dollars.

Nor was this yet all. Mr. McNamara also owned 24,250 shares of Ford stock, which, to avoid the conflict-of-interest problem, he had to sell at a time the stock market was badly depressed. From a high in the mid-nineties, Ford stock had slid down to sixty-five dollars a share. This cost Mr. McNamara another $750,000. A capital gains tax added another $250,000.

All in all, assuming that he stays in office four years, Secretary of Defense McNamara will patriotically have paid about a million dollars a year for the privilege of serving his country in a tremendously difficult and complex post—one in which a good many men have lost not only money, but their hard-earned reputations.

(As an aside, thoughtful Americans may want to consider whether it is advisable for the nation to continue to require such financial sacrifices as Messrs. McNamara and Arthur Goldberg, Secretary of Labor, and others have made. While some outstanding men have been willing to make such sacrifices, many have not, often considering such action unfair to their families. Perhaps consideration should be given to modification of the capital gains tax laws and the conflict-of-interest laws to see if some way could not be found so that the nation might avail itself of the best brains in the country without requiring them to accept such tremendous financial

50

penalties. Incidentally, Mrs. McNamara, when queried by a reporter as to how she felt about the vast reduction of her husband's salary, smiled and said, "It is plenty.")

It's interesting to note that a major concern of Mr. McNamara's in accepting the position of Secretary of Defense was not finance but his family. Secretary McNamara is a family man, who takes every opportunity to travel, vacation and just plain "have fun" with his wife and children. The McNamaras are skiing enthusiasts and, in past years, one vacation was invariably scheduled for ski resorts. Mr. McNamara's concern for his wife and family, in the move to Washington from the tranquil life of Ann Arbor, was a large one, he stated in several interviews.

Secretary of Defense Robert Strange McNamara was elected President of the Ford Motor Company the day after John Fitzgerald Kennedy was elected President of the United States. His selection was the climax of a meteoric career, begun fourteen years before as one of a group of management consultants called, sometimes in exasperation, but mostly in admiration, "the whiz kids." Mr. McNamara was the first person not a member of the Ford family to be elected president of the company.

Robert McNamara is a complex and many-sided man. As well as achieving the pinnacle of industrial success, he has been dramatically successful in such diverse roles as being a college professor and as an Army Air Force officer. He won election to Phi Beta Kappa at the conclusion of his sophomore year at the University of California, where he majored in economics and philosophy. A few years later, he was a 29-year-old lieutenant colonel in the Army Air Force.

In between, he was a scholarship student at the Harvard Graduate School of Business Administration, married his fellow classmate, Margaret Craig (he proposed to her via long-distance telephone), began a career with the top-notch accounting firm of Price Waterhouse and Company, and switched over to teaching at the Harvard Business School.

After three years of teaching at Harvard as an assistant professor of business administration, McNamara was appointed a consultant to the War Department to aid in the installation of a statistical control system for the Air Force. Later, he was commissioned as an Air Force captain, and served in England, India, China and the Pacific. He won the Legion of Merit, and, when discharged, in 1946, was a lieutenant colonel—at 29!

51

Then came the turning point of McNamara's life. With a group of nine other Air Force officers, McNamara formed a business-management team. While still in the service, the "team" had sent off scores of letters to important U. S. firms. At this point, the story takes an almost Horatio Alger-like turn. Henry Ford II, then deeply troubled about the financial position of the Ford Motor Company, which was losing money, hired the "team." In the next fourteen years, they ferreted out trouble spots in the far-flung Ford Motor Company, changed the color on the company balance sheet from red ink to black. In some awe, the long-timers in the industry dubbed them "the whiz kids."

"The whole bunch was amazing," one auto executive said. "McNamara just whizzed faster than any of the others."

Promotions came fast. McNamara managed the company's planning office and financial analysis office until 1949, when he was promoted to controller. In August, 1953, he was appointed assistant general manager of Ford Division and in January, 1955, was elected a vice president and named general manager of the division.

He was appointed vice president and group executive—car and truck divisions—on May 23, 1957, and on August 8, 1957, was elected a director of the company. Appointed to the executive committee following his election as a director, he also was a member of the company's administration committee. He was elected president of the company on November 9, 1960.

The writers asked Secretary McNamara to comment on the astonishing achievements of the "whiz kids," He laughed modestly. "It was one of those propitious moments when the company had need of a group of individuals with our particular qualifications," he told us with a smile. "Charles Thornton, President of Litton Industries, was the leader of the group. Friends put us in touch with the Ford Management."

Only a little more than three weeks after he was named Ford President, McNamara received a call from President-Elect Kennedy.

In announcing his appointment of McNamara, Mr. Kennedy reported that he had talked with many persons about the incredibly difficult job of Secretary of Defense and "Mr. McNamara's name kept coming up."

It is significant that, as in the case of another Cabinet

52

appointee, Douglas Dillon, Secretary of the Treasury, also a Republican, the President ignored politics and sought the man he believed to be best qualified for the post.

McNamara had little hesitation in accepting. "You can't put personal or company interests ahead of the national interest," he told the writers.

Being Secretary of Defense is a tough, "reputation-ruining" job. A galaxy of admirals and generals, many of them with powerful political influence on Capitol Hill, are constantly pulling and hauling in different directions. It takes a strong man to make the life-and-death decisions which the Secretary of Defense must make—and then have the courage and political know-how to put those decisions into practice. Politics in the Pentagon are murderous.

Here's how the pattern has worked in the past: When one of the services—the Army, Navy or Air Force—learns via the Pentagon grapevine that a decision is going to go against it, all hell breaks loose. Quite unofficially, but with lethal effectiveness, the new program is attacked. Disappointed generals, admirals or their aides "leak" stories to the press. They enlist powerful Congressmen to fight the order. Defense contractors and others with vested interests in fighting the decision jump into the fray. And, since decisions often cannot be proved to be right with mathematical certainty, opponents can mask their own self-interest behind claims for the national interest. The reputation of more than one Secretary of Defense has been ruined in just this kind of no-holds-barred struggle.

The first Secretary of Defense, James V. Forrestal, an ultraconscientious man, was caught in a merciless cross-fire of Pentagon politics. It drove him to a nervous breakdown and eventually to suicide.

Until the present, no Secretary of Defense has been able to really halt the interservice civil war inside the Pentagon. Former Secretary of Defense Charles E. Wilson announced, upon taking office, that he planned to "knock some heads together" among the warring generals and admirals to affect unification of the armed services. This was an admirable sentiment, but Secretary Wilson came and went—and the armed forces remained ununified.

The question in defense circles now is: "Is McNamara different?"

There seems to be considerable evidence that he is. He is a

strong and vigorous man—backed by a strong and vigorous President. Furthermore, he has an incredible mind for facts and figures. (Henry Ford II once commented: "Things most men have to turn to books and reports for, Bob carries around in his head.") One long-time Pentagon official put it bluntly: "He's smarter than any of his predecessors."

Secretary McNamara is a thorough man with a highly systematic mind. While in school, he would catalogue most of his activities. He even kept a card file of jokes suitable for classroom occasions, one friend reported. The cards neatly noted the date the joke was told, and indicated class reaction with comments such as "laughter" added.

Be that as it may, Robert McNamara quickly served notice that he plans to brook no sniping from dissidents who hope to sabotage his programs.

Secretary McNamara moved quickly to take steps to ensure this. Almost his first step was to make clear that his decisions would be final—and binding—upon the dissident admirals and generals.

"During the development of policies relating to the Defense Department, I expect full and open discussion *within the department* by all the leaders of the department, military and civilian, without regard to whether their views conform to those of others in the department, including my own," he said.

"Once a decision has been reached an a policy established representing the decisions of the President or other appropriate authorities, then all members of the department, civilian and military, will be expected to support that decision, publicly and otherwise."

Another important step taken by Robert McNamara was the speeding up—by an estimated four years—of the delivery of troop transport planes. Under this schedule, jet troop planes are ready to rush U. S. infantrymen anywhere on the globe within hours. "Small wars" of the "brush-fire" variety require this instant mobility.

Scarcely two months after he took office, McNamara made a decision of vast importance—awarding the bulk of future space development to the Air Force.

As might have been expected, an explosion promptly followed.

A story was "leaked" (by person or persons unknown) to the Chicago *Sun-Times* to the effect that General Lyman Lemnitzer, Chairman of the Joint Chiefs of Staff, felt this basic decision had been taken without sufficient consultation with the Joint Chiefs—and strongly implying that the step endangered national security.

For once, the parties playing this kind of typical Pentagon politics seem to have overreached themselves—thanks in large part to prompt action by General Lemnitzer. The story, the general testified before a hearing of the House Armed Services Committee, was based upon a confidential memorandum prepared by him at the request of Secretary McNamara. Furthermore, it was written *before*—not *after*—the Secretary of Defense issued his order. Most of his objections, the general testified, had been met by permitting the Army and Navy to retain space projects then under development. Whoever "leaked" the story, General Lemnitzer testified hotly, was, in his opinion, guilty of "treasonable" conduct.

The entire incident seemed to strengthen—rather than weaken—McNamara's hand. This is one of the few times such a result had occurred. It tends to strengthen the widespread impression that the Secretary of Defense is a very smart and resourceful man, indeed.

When the authors questioned Secretary McNamara about Pentagon politics and interservice rivalries, he seemed not unduly concerned about them. "This disturbed me greatly when I first came here," he told us candidly, "and it's true that you don't meet anything quite like this in private business. The whole subject of interservice rivalries is difficult to appraise. So far, I don't believe it has had a damaging effect —but, of course, it could if it gets out of hand."

Secretary McNamara was smiling and quietly confident as he spoke. Without braggadocio, it was evident that he feels he can control the dissidents.

Like the other members of the Kennedy Cabinet, Mr. McNamara is a tremendously hard worker.

"We understand that you begin your work day at seven in the morning, Mr. Secretary," the writers said.

"Not quite that early," Mr. McNamara smiled. "But I'm usually here by seven-fifteen in the morning. My hours are about the same as at Ford—perhaps a little longer."

"Here" is a spacious office on the third floor of the Pentagon, decorated with charming pastel landscapes on the wall and a ruby-red carpet on the floor. Behind his immense desk hangs a portrait of James Forrestal, the first Secretary of Defense. A row of floor-to-ceiling windows flank one wall.

From his window, Secretary McNamara can see a dramatic

55

view of Washington across the Potomac River. Below him are the serenity of the Tidal Basin and the Jefferson Memorial. Above the beige draperies are cornices, each topped by an impressive bronze eagle.

In the alcove to his office is a dramatic, World War II era painting showing an amphibious naval landing craft invading a war-torn beach. On a heavy, ornately carved, dark wooden table behind Secretary McNamara's desk stands the familiar white telephone. It is a direct line to the White House. Similar white telephones stand on the desks of all Cabinet members and other key administration officials.

Mr. McNamara spends most of his time in his offices these days. With crises in Laos, the Congo, Berlin and other strife-torn spots, he is confined closely to his post. There is a wry saying in the Pentagon that "McNamara can get more done in an eighteen-hour day than most people can in a twenty-four-hour one." It's indicative of the tremendous responsibilities placed on top Defense officials.

On the lighter side, Secretary McNamara reports he has been taking some good-natured kidding because he is driven to and from work in a Cadillac, the product of the Ford Motor Company's closest competitor, General Motors. The Cadillacs are loaned at low rental to the government by the auto company through General Services Administration.

There's one story told about the former Ford President that indicates that the highly intellectual Phi Beta Kappa Robert McNamara had limited mechanical ability. According to the story, one damp morning Mr. McNamara's Ford refused to start and he had to call on his wife for help. Mrs. McNamara came to her husband's aid by lifting the hood of the car, wiping off the wet spark plugs, and sending him off to Detroit with the words: "Try it now."

The writers asked Mr. McNamara how his life had changed since he had exchanged the presidency of the Ford Motor Company for the post of Secretary of Defense.

"The problems I deal with now are broader and more varied," the Secretary of Defense responded "The answers are usually more ill-defined and less certain than in private business. Problems are complicated by the addition of Congress, the press and the public as parties to their solution. And there is certainly far more controversy about any suggested solution."

Mr. McNamara was then asked to describe his main objectives as Secretary of Defense.

56

"The first objective is, of course, to carry out the President's mandate to strengthen the nation's military posture," he replied. "This is a prerequisite to achieving a peace we haven't enjoyed in recent years. This requires many things: determining force levels, assessing weapons systems, both those of our country and those of our allies in world-wide alliances, conducting research and development, and, of course, formulating a policy for the future.

"Then, of course," the Secretary added, "you have to translate all of these things into reality. . . to see that the work agreed on is actually done. That requires proper programs and controls."

The Secretary noted that task forces had been hard at work on "more than 120 projects in which parts of these objectives are involved." In total, these 120-plus projects represent a reappraisal of the nation's entire defense strategy.

The awesome problems with which Mr. McNamara deals were suggested at one of his appearances before the House of Representatives Armed Services Committee. One of the main facets of defense planning, the Secretary said on that occasion, was "survivability"—the ability to strike a "decisive counterblow" by American forces even after a possible enemy attack by intercontinental ballistic missiles. The theory is, of course, that if the United States possesses the ability to retaliate even after a surprise attack, the attack is much less likely to come.

"No effort should be spared, no measure overlooked, which can reasonably be expected to contribute to the strengthening, protection and sure control of these crucial retaliatory forces," McNamara told the Congressmen.

"Particularly, we must emphasize those weapons systems which inherently have, or can be provided with, a high degree of survivability under a massive intercontinental ballistic missile attack."

In his congressional appearance, the Secretary of Defense laid special stress on the Polaris atomic-powered submarine. This highly mobile weapon, loaded with sixteen nuclear-powered missiles which can be launched from under the sea, provides a powerful deterrent to an attack upon the United States. Even if America were hit, Polaris-type submarines would retain the power to strike back with devastating force. Thus, they discourage attack in the first place.

As he feared, Secretary McNamara's awesome responsibilities have cut down on the amount of time he can spend

57

with his family. The McNamaras have two daughters, Margaret, 19, and Kathleen, 16, and a son, Craig, 10. Kathy climbed the fabulous Matterhorn at the age of 12. "One of the youngest ever to do it, I believe," the Secretary of Defense smiles.

One of the family hobbies is travel. The Secretary had a wandering foot, even as a boy. He signed aboard as an ordinary seaman and traveled to the Panama Canal, Hawaii and the Orient before he was 21 years old, despite the anxiety of his parents. Living in the seaport city of San Francisco proved too great a lure to resist for a young man anxious to see the world.

For relaxation, Secretary McNamara prefers reading. He is an omnivorous reader, devouring books on history, current events, politics and even mathematics and statistics.

Deputy Secretary of Defense Roswell L. Gilpatric

Deputy Secretary Gilpatric is the number two man at Defense and helps carry the burden inherent in the top executive jobs in this largest and most complex of all government departments.

He left private law practice with the New York City firm of Cravath, Swaine and Moore to accept his present position. He has had a distinguished career in business, government and academic life. During World War II, Mr. Gilpatric worked on war production contract problems of the government—working closely with the Navy, Air Force and the Defense Plant Corporation on finance and emergency plant facilities. From 1951 to 1953, he was successively Assistant Secretary and Under Secretary of the Air Force.

Secretary of the Navy John Connally, Jr.

Secretary Connally had a brilliant Navy career in service during World War II. He entered the service as an ensign in June, 1941, and served until October, 1945, when he was relieved from active duty as a lieutenant commander. During his Navy career, he served in the office of the Chief of Naval Operations and in the office of the Under Secretary of the Navy, where he dealt with problems of training and manpower, now one of his primary responsibilities. His boss was James Forrestal, then an Under Secretary of the Navy.

Secretary Connally's job includes direction of both the Navy and the Marine Corps and "such aviation as may be organic therein," reads a Pentagon directive. His primary duties, as in the Department of the Army, are concerned with training, equipping and organizing naval forces. His jurisdiction mainly concerns operations at sea and such land operations as are necessary to conduct a naval campaign and such air support as is necessary to support essential naval operations.

Secretary of the Army Elvis Jacob Stahr, Jr.

Secretary Stahr, true to the New Frontier "clan," is a Phi Beta Kappa and a Rhodes Scholar. He served as a Special Assistant to Secretary of the Army Frank Pace, Jr., during the Korean War. He also held posts in the previous Eisenhower Administration, serving as the Executive Director of the President's Committee on Education Beyond High School. He was a member of President-Elect Kennedy's task force on depressed areas, serving under the Chairmanship of Senator Paul Douglas of Illinois, prior to his present post.

During World War II, Secretary Stahr rolled up an impressive record in the Far Eastern theater, winning seven medals and many battle stars and ribbons, while rising in rank from second lieutenant to lieutenant colonel. Secretary Stahr was on combat duty in China for many months during the war and became interested in the Chinese language. He later won a diploma in Chinese language from Yale University.

Secretary of the Air Force Eugene M. Zuckert

Secretary Zuckert, like his counterparts in the Navy and the Army, is a lawyer and has had wide government service. He was once an assistant in the Department of War for Air prior to the existence of the Air Force as a separate department. Mr Zuckert was, in fact, the first Assistant Secretary of the Air Force, taking his oath of office in September, 1947, during the Truman Administration. His superior was the first Secretary of the Air Force—Stuart Symington, now Missouri's senior United States Senator.

From 1937 to 1940, Secretary Zuckert was Attorney for the U. S. Securities and Exchange Commission. After his service in the fledgling Department of the Air Force, he was a member of the U. S. Atomic Energy Commission for several years. He "retired" to private life in 1954 to become an atomic energy consultant and attorney.

Assistant Secretary of Defense Carlisle P. Runge (Manpower)

Mr. Runge's post covers problems involved in civilian and

military personnel, their medical, educational and health requirements, internal and industrial security, and reserve programs and policies of the Defense establishment.

He is an attorney, a graduate of the University of Wisconsin Law School, and he also attended school at Oxford, England. From 1951 to the present, he was associated with the faculty of the University of Wisconsin as a professor of law and the Co-ordinator of the University's National Securities Study Group.

Assistant Secretary of Defense Charles Hitch (Comptroller)

Mr. Hitch's duties are primarily in management and other related housekeeping jobs, such as accounting, weapons systems evaluation and management evaluation. Prior to entering government service, he had been with the Rand Corporation, a firm of scientific consultants.

During World War II, Mr. Hitch served as an aide to Ambassador Averell Harriman on the first Lend-Lease Mission in London in 1941-42. He entered active duty in 1943, and was assigned to the Office of Strategic Services as an Army officer. He later served as Chief of the Stabilization Controls Division of the Office of War Mobilization and Reconversion.

Mr. Hitch received his undergraduate degree from the University of Arizona, did a year's graduate work at Harvard, and then went on to Oxford as a Rhodes Scholar.

Assistant Secretary of Defense Thomas D. Morris (Installations and Logistics)

A University of Tennessee graduate, Mr. Morris is no newcomer to the Department of Defense or to government service. In 1956-57 he served in several capacities in the department, including the position as Deputy Assistant Secretary for Supply and Logistics, an office now merged with the office he heads. Maintenance policy, planning and supply management are all part of the over-all duties of Installations and Logistics.

Prior to returning to the Department of Defense, Mr. Morris served as an Assistant Director for Management in the Bureau of the Budget. During World War II, he was in the Navy and was a member of the Navy Management Engineering Staff. He has participated in both of the Hoover Commissions' studies and has conducted management surveys for a number of federal agencies and private organizations.

Assistant Secretary of Defense Paul Henry Nitze
(International Security Affairs)

Mr. Nitze works closely with Presidential Assistant Mc-George Bundy and with Department of State in the entire field of security around the world. His defense position is concerned also with duties of foreign military rights and military assistance and with foreign economic affairs in the international military fields.

Mr. Nitze has been in and out of government, private business and academic life during his career. He has served in the Department of State and, prior to taking his Defense Department post, was President of the Foreign Service Educational Foundation and an Associate of the Washington Center of Foreign Policy Research of the School of Advanced International Studies. He was Vice Chairman of the United States Strategic Bombing Survey during World War II, and is a graduate of Harvard with a B.A. degree *cum laude*.

Assistant Secretary of Defense Arthur Sylvester
(Public Affairs)

A Princeton man, Mr. Sylvester supervises the vast news service activities of the department as well as declassification, public affairs programs, and other allied public relations services of the highly technical, security-conscious department.

Mr. Sylvester has been a newspaperman most of his life. Most recently he was correspondent and bureau chief of the Newark (New Jersey) *News*, stationed in Washington, D.C.

CHAPTER FOUR

C. Douglas Dillon and the Treasury Department

THE OFFICE——The Secretary of the Treasury is the chief adviser to the President on fiscal affairs. He has both administrative and policy-determining responsibilities in the management of the country's finances, and he exercises authority on many phases of foreign financial policy.

The Treasury Department maintains field organizations in all of the states and has offices in most principal cities across the nation. The main Treasury Building is a handsome five-story Greek Revival granite structure across the street from the White House.

Ionic columns, each an impressive thirty-six feet high, surround the building's outside perimeter. Inside, fluted Corinthian pilasters, topped by capitals bearing the eagle and the key of the Treasury seal, stand sentry duty in the broad marble corridors of the building. To the south of the building stands a statue of Alexander Hamilton, first Secretary of the Treasury. At the north entrance stands a bronze statue of Albert Gallatin, the fourth Secretary of the Treasury.

Beginnings of the Treasury date back to the Second Continental Congress. In July, 1775, a joint responsibility for managing the finance of the Revolutionary government of the infant provisional United States was fixed. Joint treasurers were Michael Hillegas and George Clymers, who set up offices in Philadelphia and posted a bond "in the sum of 100,000 dollars" as "surety for the faithful performance of their office." By April, 1776, Congress set up a closely supervised system of managing the finances of the country.

With the adoption of the Declaration of Independence on July 4, 1776, the newly established United States of America entered the international credit mart—as a borrower. That autumn the Treasury recommended the borrowing of "five hundred thousand dollars for the use of the United States," and Congress agreed and fixed the rate of interest at 4 per cent.

For a brief period in the pre-Constitutional days of the union, the Treasury Office ceased to function when Robert Morris of Pennsylvania, a signer of the Declaration of Independence, was named Superintendent of Finance. The Congress put the nation's "Financier" in charge of the fiscal responsibilities of the nation and as top management of the Department of the Navy. In September, 1789, the Treasury Department, as we know it, was established under the Constitution.

Alexander Hamilton, Washington's former aide-de-camp, was appointed Secretary of the Treasury on September 11, 1789. At 32, he was a prominent lawyer of New York City and had taken an active role in the framing of the Constitution of the United States.

Hamilton's brilliant performance, in organizing, coordinating and expanding his duties, was legendary even in his own time. His first report to Congress shows a remarkable grasp of the importance of sound fiscal planning of the nation's resources.

He said, in part: "The debt of the United States . . . was the price of liberty. . . . The faith of America was pledged for it, and with solemnities that gave peculiar force to the obligation. . . . While the observation of that good faith which is the basis of the public credit is recommended by the strongest inducements of political expediency, it is enforced by consideration of still greater authority, the immutable principles of moral obligation."

Albert Gallatin was appointed to the office by President Thomas Jefferson. He served longer than any other Treasury Secretary, from 1801 to 1814, under Jefferson and President James Madison. Both Hamilton and Gallatin were born outside of the continental limits of the United States, Hamilton in the West Indies, Gallatin in Switzerland. They are the only two of the fifty-five Secretaries of the Treasury not to have been native Americans.

The basic working structure as originally established in the Constitution and expanded by these early fiscal pioneers has remained sufficiently malleable to meet the day-to-day needs of the government down to the present time. The office of the Secretary and that of the Treasurer of the United States still retain most of their original characteristics and duties, though periodic reorganizations and changes of duties and authorities have taken place. The Treasury once supervised the Postal Service, the General Land Office (now the Department of the Interior) and many operations of business that have since become duties of the Departments of Commerce and of Labor. The contemporary structure of the Treasury is vaster in scope, with its sphere of action extending beyond the borders of our country with representatives in major U. S. embassies around the world.

Today the Secretary of the Treasury is United States Governor of the International Bank for Reconstruction and Development, the International Monetary Fund and the Inter-American Development Bank. He is a member of the Loan Policy Board of the Small Business Administration, Foreign-Trade Zones Board, Joint Committee on Reduction of Nonessential Federal Expenditures, Board of Trustees of the Postal Savings System, Smithsonian Institution, Board of Trustees of the National Gallery of Art, National Park Trust Fund Board, the Foreign Service Buildings Commission and the Commission on Intergovernmental Relations. The Secretary is also Honorary Treasurer of the American National Red Cross.

On the interdepartmental level, the Secretary of the Treasury is: (1) Chairman of the National Advisory Council on International Monetary and Financial Problems, which coordinates the policies and operations of government agencies which make or participate in the making of foreign loans or engage in foreign financial exchange or monetary transactions; (2) Managing Trustee of the Federal Old-Age and Survivors Insurance Trust Fund, which manages the fund from which Social Security benefits are paid; (3) Chairman of the Library of Congress Trust Fund Board, which accepts, holds and administers gifts, bequests or devises of property for the Library.

The Secretary is a busy man indeed!

There are several vestiges of nonmonetary activities still under the authority of the Secretary of the Treasury as established by the Founding Fathers. One of these is the Coast Guard of the United States.

The background of the Coast Guard in the Treasury Department is an especially interesting one because the service is a branch of the military in times of war, but a wing of the Treasury in times of peace unless the President directs otherwise.

It is the oldest continuous U. S. naval service and was organized under President George Washington in 1790 as the Revenue Marine, with ten cutters at its disposal. It has grown into a service for most coastal waters problems of the country and includes such diverse activities as port security, aids to navigation, inspection of merchant vessels, weather bureau information gathering, small boating safety, search and rescue work, the operation of the Ice Patrol and Ice Observation services and many other government services to shipping.

Other Treasury activities include:

The Bureau of the Public Debt—which handles the administration of government bonds and other forms of the public debt.

The Office of the Comptroller of the Currency—which has supervision over all national banks.

The Internal Revenue Service—which is responsible for the determination, assessment and collection of all internal revenue, individual and corporate income taxes and all miscellaneous taxes.

The Bureau of Engraving and Printing—which engraves and prints currency, bonds, postage stamps, cigarette and liquor stamps and the like.

64

Bureau of the Mint—which makes and distributes coins, safeguards the government's gold, silver and other monetary metals, makes medals for the armed services and performs similar tasks.

Office of International Finance—which assists the Secretary in international financial and monetary matters.

Division of Foreign Assets Control—administers regulations issued by the Secretary under the Trading with the Enemy Act, which control transactions with foreign nationals.

Office of Defense Lending—which carries out the provisions of the Reconstruction Finance Liquidation Act of 1953 and related statutes.

The Bureau of the Customs—dates back to Colonial times. At one time it provided the principal, if not the only, tax revenues levied by the federal government. It collects duties on imported items, prevents smuggling, supervises the importation and entry of merchandise and baggage, and the clearance and unloading of vessels, aircraft and vehicles from foreign countries.

The Narcotics Bureau—regulates and governs the use of narcotics.

The Secret Service—suppresses counterfeiting, guards the safety of the President of the United States and his immediate family, investigates the forgery of government checks and bonds, and enforces a wide variety of other federal laws.

THE MAN——C. Douglas Dillon is *the* man everybody likes. Perhaps more than that, he is the man in whose cool, dispassionate, slightly Olympian judgment all of Washington trusts. He has the habit of being right, of spotting problems long before others do, and pointing out solutions before the problems have even occurred to most others.

His appointment as Secretary of the Treasury by Democratic President-Elect Kennedy was announced at a time when he was serving in the second-highest office in the State Department—Under Secretary—during the administration of Republican President Dwight Eisenhower.

Douglas Dillon is an unrepentent Republican in the midst of President Kennedy's Democratic Cabinet. At his first press conference, a reporter asked Secretary Dillon how he, a Republican, felt working in the Kennedy Administration.

With his shy smile, Dillon peered benignly at his questioner from behind his horn-rimmed glasses. He said quietly he felt "highly congenial."

Asked if he still called himself a Republican, the Secretary of the Treasury smiled again and replied: "I certainly do."

There was some slight grousing by a few ultraconservative Republicans when Douglas Dillon joined the Kennedy Cabinet as Secretary of the Treasury. It was widely assumed that, had Richard Nixon won the Presidency, Mr. Dillon would have been his Secretary of the Treasury—or perhaps Secretary of State. A few Republicans saw Dillon's appointment as a sinister Democratic plot to obscure "party responsibility"— and to have a Republican handy as a scapegoat in case the fiscal programs of the Kennedy Administration turned sour.

But these few voices in the wilderness were drowned out in a chorus of approval. Perhaps more than any other single man in Washington, Secretary of the Treasury Douglas Dillon commands virtually universal respect and admiration.

The writers asked him if there were any historical parallels to the unprecedented compliment paid to him.

"Oh, yes," he said earnestly. "Henry Stimson is an example that comes to mind at once." (Mr. Stimson served as Secretary of War under Republican President William Howard Taft, as Secretary of State during the administration of Republican Herbert Hoover, and as Secretary of War in the Cabinet of Democrat Franklin Delano Roosevelt.)

"I think," Secretary Dillon continued, referring to his own appointment, "that it is only the continuity of service that is unusual. The situation was special. Apparently the President felt there was a crisis of confidence. He felt that my background in the State Department would be helpful in the Treasury."

"Have you found your experience with the State Department helpful to you as Secretary of the Treasury?" we asked.

"Very much so," the Secretary replied in quiet, carefully measured words. "Developments which have recently taken place in the world require the Treasury Department to be intimately aware of—and to pay close attention to—what is going on in the rest of the world. The return of currency convertibility for the first time since the twenties and early thirties . . . the tremendous problems facing us in connection with assistance development in foreign countries . . . our foreign policy is closely tied in with fiscal considerations and the two must be closely co-ordinated."

Clarence Douglas Dillon was born in Switzerland—in the League of Nations City of Geneva—on August 21, 1901. His father, Clarence Dillon, founder of the giant investment firm of Dillon, Read and Company, was one of the fabulous figures of Wall Street during the 1920's—when tax rates were low and it was possible to make a fortune and keep it. The elder Dillon's career is evidence of the fabulous Land of Opportunity that is America. His father was a Polish immigrant boy named Samuel Lapowski. Coming to Abilene, Texas, to start a store, the ambitious young man adopted his mother's maiden name—Dillon. He did very well—well enough to send his son, the father of the present Treasury Secretary, to Harvard. Clarence Dillon parlayed what he learned at Harvard into one of America's most fabulous fortunes, estimated at upward of half a billion dollars.

One of the legends of Wall Street involves a personal check written by the Secretary's father—for the staggering sum of *one hundred and forty-six million dollars!* It represented the purchase price of the Dodge Auto Company by a financial syndicate headed by Clarence Dillon.

In his senior year at Harvard—from which he graduated number one in his class—young Douglas Dillon wooed and won the beautiful Phyllis Ellsworth, one of Boston's prettiest belles. Today, Mrs. Dillon is one of the handsomest women in Washington.

His education at Groton and Harvard finished, Douglas Dillon purchased a seat on the New York Stock Exchange for $185,000 and entered upon a career as a Wall Street investment banker.

Even the long-timers of Wall Street were amazed by young Douglas' razor-keen mind. His memory for intricate facts and figures is legendary. Highlights of his long and varied career as an investment banker include the Presidency of the United States and Foreign Securities Corporation, the Board Chairmanship of Dillon, Read and Company, and participation in the financial affairs of companies all over the world.

(In preparation for becoming Secretary of the Treasury, Mr. Dillon disposed of his entire stocks in the family concern of Dillon, Read and Company—"because the company is in the business of buying and selling and underwriting securities, and while in that business . . . from time to time they buy and sell and operate in the area of municipal and state securities.")

The future Secretary of the Treasury's Wall Street career was interrupted by four years of active service with the Navy during World War II. In 1941, he was commissioned an ensign. In 1945, he was released from active duty as a lieutenant commander. For his services at the bloody fighting of Guam, Saipan and in the Philippines, Dillon received the Legion of Merit and the Air Medal.

After the war, Dillon found himself attracted to politics— as an active Republican.

In his early days, Dillon was considered a protégé of his long-time friend, the late Secretary of State John Foster Dulles, who "discovered" or helped advance the careers of many notable diplomats and prominent figures in the Kennedy Administration, including Secretary of State Dean Rusk.

Mr. Dillon was associated with Mr. Dulles in advising GOP candidate Thomas E. Dewey on foreign affairs in 1948. Mr. Dewey unexpectedly lost to Harry S. Truman, but four years later, the future Secretary of the Treasury picked a winner. A liberal Republican, he vigorously supported the nomination of Dwight D. Eisenhower against Robert A. Taft in 1952. Upon the former's election, Dillon was named United States Ambassador to France.

In France, Dillon was popular. He and his family speak French fluently. He also has a passion for art. (In his outer office hangs an original, brilliantly colored Vlaminck. In his six homes, he has an outstanding collection of paintings by Renoir, Degas, Monet, Manet, and other Impressionist and Post-Impressionist painters.) The cultivated French admired Ambassador Dillon's artistic bent—and also his reputation as a connoisseur of fine foods and wines.

The Secretary of the Treasury owns one of the finest vineyards in France—the Château Haut-Brion. It produces a rich, red Bordeaux wine that is annually rated among the world's best. Dillon once remarked to an aide that he could, by taste alone, identify the year a given glass of Bordeaux was produced *or* the vineyard which produced the grapes from which the wine came.

"But," he added modestly, "I can't tell the year *and* the vineyard, the way some experts can."

The writers asked Mr. Dillon about his reputation as a linguist. He modestly demurred that it was much overrated. "French is the only language besides English that I speak reasonably well," he said with a quiet laugh.

An aide was sitting with us in the leather-bound chairs around an informal coffee table in the Secretary's six-hundred-square-foot office. "Don't you speak German, too?" he asked Mr. Dillon in surprise.

The Secretary of the Treasury shook his head. "That goes

68

a long way back," he said somewhat regretfully. "All the way back to my youth. I'm afraid I don't really know German any more."

Ambassador Dillon's service in France coincided with some of the thorniest American-French diplomatic problems in many years—including the Suez crisis (during which America denounced the French invasion of Egypt in the United Nations); the Indochina crisis, which saw France lose her empire in Southeast Asia, and the admission of France's traditional enemy—West Germany—into the North Atlantic Treaty Organization.

Nevertheless, Ambassador Dillon's skill as a diplomat kept U. S.-French ties reasonably intact.

Impressed by Dillon's skill and breadth of economic experience, Secretary Dulles recalled him to Washington, and President Eisenhower promoted him to the unsung, but key, position of Under Secretary of State for Economic Affairs— the third-ranking post in the State Department. His mission— to promote trade and co-ordinate mutual assistance among the free nations of the world.

One of Secretary Dillon's many "brain children," which illustrates the close relationship between his work in the State Department and his present post as Treasury Secretary, is the Organization for Economic Co-operation and Development. Sometimes called the Dillon Plan, this treaty links Western Europe, Canada and the United States with close economic ties and aims to undertake mutually the program of providing aid to underdeveloped countries.

OECD is the successor to the old Organization for European Economic Co-operation "which was originally established in 1948 to assist in carrying out the Marshall Plan," the Secretary of the Treasury explained. "The old organization had completed the task it was designed to fulfill. Western Europe had been restored to vigorous health. Discriminatory trade quotas were rapidly disappearing. Convertibility of the major European currencies had been re-established."

Now we are entering upon a new era and face new challenges, Mr. Dillon notes.

"In this era, intra-European co-operation remains important and must be preserved. But, beyond this, the industrialized countries of Western Europe and North America must work in full partnership, to strengthen the economy of the entire free world and to provide the developing countries with the resources they so sorely need."

69

By the fall of 1959, Mr. Dillon's idea for a new economic alliance between Western Europe, Canada and the United States had matured to the point where President Eisenhower, Chancellor Adenauer of West Germany, President de Gaulle of France and Prime Minister Macmillan of Great Britain held four-power talks about OECD. Negotiations followed between the eighteen member countries of the old OEEC, the U. S. and Canada. A charter was drafted for the successor organization. In appearing before the Senate Foreign Relations Committee to urge U. S. ratification, Mr. Dillon noted that two functions of OECD are of vital importance to the Treasury Department: "those that will invigorate our economy and those that will improve our balance of payments position.

"For the first time in over thirty years, and to a larger extent than ever before in our history, our success in pursuing these objectives is dependent on the understanding and cooperation of the industrialized countries of Western Europe. In turn, their economies are heavily influenced by our actions. . . . We must take into account the international repercussions of actions which we take . . . since the reactions they may provoke abroad could easily frustrate our objectives. The only answer is close, continuing consultation and cooperation with Canada and the countries of Western Europe. The OECD is designed to provide the forum for this consultation and co-operation."

The OECD or Dillon Plan is also expected to ease the burden of foreign aid, which America has shouldered almost alone for many years.

Secretary Dillon is a quiet, unassuming man who tends closely to his work. He isn't particularly keen about getting his name in the newspapers—rare in Washington where every other person you meet is a publicity hound. He does in quiet ways things which from anyone else would be very grand gestures, indeed.

Take, for instance, the matter of the $40,000 crystal chandeliers which now adorn the glittering new State Department Building. Congress refused to appropriate the necessary money to pay for them. Dillon, then Under Secretary of State, quietly paid for them himself and donated them to the State Department.

One reason Douglas Dillon is so universally respected is that his keen mind quickly discerns possible trouble spots in our national economy.

Take, for example, the matter of America's economic "growth." For years, Dillon has been preaching that America has not been growing fast enough—and this at a time only a few public figures and supposedly ivory-tower economics professors were worrying about the matter. Speaking before the Harvard Alumni Association in 1959, Mr. Dillon urged that the government and private business exert their utmost efforts to encourage a national economic growth rate of 5 per cent annually. On many other occasions before and afterward, he plugged for an increased rate of growth to keep the American economy running full tilt.

Most of Mr. Dillon's fellow Republicans paid little attention, but his ideas were vigorously shared by Democrat John F. Kennedy. During the Presidential election campaign of 1960, Democratic Candidate Kennedy kept hammering away at the "lagging" rate of growth in America. Republican Candidate Nixon, on the other hand, dismissed such talk as "Growthmanship" early in the race.

"It is very important for America to maintain a maximum rate of growth," Secretary Dillon told the writers. "This can be done without inflation. The countries of Western Europe have been able to maintain more rapid rates of growth and to avoid inflation. We certainly must grow fast enough to absorb our labor force so that we will have full employment."

He also stressed the need for tax reform—and the relationship between tax policy, growth and prosperity.

"In my opinion," Mr. Dillon said, "substantial tax reform is needed. I think the Treasury has something to contribute to the matter of economic growth, for instance. Monetary and tax policy are very important here. We need a tax climate that gives greater stimulus to effort and growth. Individual income tax rates are too high. The so-called tax 'loopholes' were created, I think, because there is a realization that tax rates are too high. By closing loopholes and dropping the tax rates, we would have a healthier climate for growth."

The vast impact of U. S. tax laws upon prosperity and employment was brought out in a fascinating exchange between Senator Albert Gore of Tennessee and Secretary Dillon during the hearings on his confirmation:

SENATOR GORE: I would like to inquire as to your views, Mr. Dillon, on questions of international economics. . . . I have been considerably disturbed at the rate and magnitude of the

71

outflow of U. S. capital, particularly for manufacturing facilities abroad. . . .

By way of preface I would like to call to your attention the fact that almost one-fifth of the capital expenditures of U. S. businesses last year, according to indications I have been able to get, were made in foreign countries. . . .

I think this is a problem which will require your attention and the attention of the country, else we may find the American labor movement becoming strong advocates of a high protective tariff, which, I think, would be a very deleterious thing not only to our own economy but, perhaps, disastrous to the free world economy. . . .

I would like to cite to you a few specific examples. In 1960 the Goodyear Tire & Rubber Co. expected to spend approximately one-half of its expenditures for plant and equipment on plants abroad; General Motors expected to spend $200 million for oversea plants; Firestone has been spending 25 to 30 per cent of its capital outlay on plants abroad; Kaiser Aluminum expected 80 per cent of its total capital outlay for 1960 to be spent on its foreign operations . . . all U. S. typewriter corporation businesses are now manufacturing their typewriters in foreign subsidiaries or branches.

Now this is encouraged very materially by tax incentives, preferential tax treatment of profits earned abroad, which form a powerful incentive for this outflow of U. S. capital.

U. S. investment abroad has more than doubled during the Eisenhower administration. It has almost trebled in the last 10 years. The outflow of capital exceeds our loss of gold.

I solicit your views on this problem.

MR. DILLON: My views on this problem, Senator, are tied in with the balance-of-payments situation which, as we recognize, is of crucial importance to our country and to the whole free world today . . . our tax laws, as presently drawn, do encourage investment abroad. They do allow specifically for the retention of earnings, the reinvestment of earnings abroad in foreign subsidiaries of American corporations, with no U. S. tax until they are repatriated.

This policy was probably adopted, and would seem to have been the proper policy, in the era when we were trying to build up the strength of Europe, or Western Europe after the war.

That strength has now been built up, and certainly I can see no particular reason, no reason at all, for special treatment to induce American capital to go to Europe and to make investments there, particularly in manufacturing industries. . . .

There are, in addition, some specific situations . . . where they have the so-called tax havens in Europe, where there is very little, if any, tax, and an American company can set up a subsidiary in a European country, manufacture there, and pay no tax either in the country where it is operating or in the

United States by simply transferring its profits as a management fee into a corporation in one of these tax-haven countries that has very little tax.

SENATOR GORE: That is generally referred to as a third country operation.

MR. DILLON: Third country operation. That type of thing I think certainly should be looked at. . . .

Dillon's quiet, diplomatic approach has served him well at one of the most harrowing trials a member of the President's Cabinet faces—testifying before congressional committees. The main joy in life of some Congressmen and Senators seems to be in bullyragging witnesses—and the more distinguished the witness, the better some congressional inquisitors relish taking him over the jumps.

"They don't do this with Secretary Dillon very much though," one of his aides remarked. "In the first place, he's highly respected by both parties. Also, he does his homework and knows what he's talking about so thoroughly that those who try to bait him quickly end up looking pretty foolish. He never tries to make them look that way, but after a little but it's so obvious that Mr. Dillon knows more about what he's talking about than they do that not many of them try to give him a bad time."

Dillon bends over backward to see the other person's point of view. One of his favorite sayings is: "You have to be understanding. The rougher you are, the rougher they are."

This attitude has spared him many a tough political battle.

One of Dillon's top assistants told the writers that the best phrase he's ever seen to describe the Secretary's fiscal policy is: "He respects the dollar without worshiping it."

Secretary Dillon's office in the ornate, old-fashioned, but handsome Old Treasury Building is small by the standards of Cabinet Secretaries. (Only Labor Secretary Goldberg's is smaller.) Still, it does have 600 square feet of floor space, so there is plenty of room to move about in. Almost square, the room has a deep red Persian carpet on the floor and elegant gold draperies at its high windows. A handsome portrait of Albert Gallatin adorns the wall above his desk.

Douglas Dillon is an athletic man whose hands still slightly bear the calluses of sailing ropes from the days—now past—when he was a champion sailor. (He has since substituted golf for sailing as his favorite exercise.) Tall, slightly balding, with a quiet, almost shy air, he towers an inch and a half over the six-foot mark. He dresses conservatively and looks like a banker's banker.

On a typical day, he might wear a dark, pin-striped blue suit (tailored in Britain) and a dark blue tie with white polka dots. He usually wears dark, horn-rimmed glasses. It is hard to imagine a sounder-looking man from the business point of view. The sight of Douglas Dillon at Treasury and Luther Hodges at Commerce has done much to quiet the fears of businessmen about the feared fiscal irresponsibility of the Kennedy Administration.

It is the consensus among Washington newsmen that Secretary Dillon is one of the persons especially close to President Kennedy. "They think very much alike," one newsman said. "Dillon is a very sound man in both finance and diplomacy. The President seeks his advice often and generally follows it."

At the writers' request, Secretary Dillon reminisced about the first time he ever met John F. Kennedy. "It was at a Harvard alumni reunion, in the autumn of 1956," Mr. Dillon said. "My twenty-fifth anniversary reunion, in fact. My classmates chose me to be Chief Marshal of the event—and one of the people getting an Honorary Degree was then Senator Kennedy. He and I had both been members of the same club at Harvard—the Spee Club. We became acquainted then and have been friends ever since."

Interestingly enough, although Douglas Dillon, as Secretary of the Treasury, is the leading banker for the entire free world, at home it is the handsome, dark-eyed Mrs. Dillon who balances the family checkbook and pays the family bills.

A graduate of the elite Mrs. Porter's finishing school at Farmington, Connecticut, Mrs. Dillon shares her husband's enthusiasm for art. One of the Dillon family hobbies is golf —which they frequently play together.

The Dillons have two married daughters, Phyllis (Mrs. Mark Collins) and Joan (Mrs. Dillon Moseley), and four grandchildren. The Dillons met while he was a student at Harvard and a friend brought him to her house for tea. After that, the future Secretary of the Treasury was a regular caller at the Ellsworth home. The popular Miss Ellsworth had numerous other suitors and, according to family legend, it was young Douglas' habit at teas and parties to wait until the others had departed and then invite her out afterward. They were married during his senior year at Harvard.

The Dillons are among the very top echelon of Washington society and go to comparatively few parties. Their home in

Washington is furnished in exquisite French antiques, and is graced by two Renoirs, a Manet, and other paintings.

They have a New York apartment, a resort home at Hobe Sound, Florida, a château in France, and a Caribbean Island hideaway as well. Their Hobe Sound home is their "dream home," Mrs. Dillon has said. The Dillons sometimes feel a sense of frustration that they are able to spend so little time in it. Mrs. Dillon spent five years in furnishing and decorating it "in exquisite female summer resort style," an aide reports, and they plan to retire there when the Secretary's work in Washington is finished.

Treasurer of the United States Elizabeth Rudel Smith

Mrs. Smith holds an office created by the first session of the United States Congress in 1789, at the time the Treasury Department was established. The basic operation of the Treasurer has remained the same as it was when first organized— "to receive and keep all moneys of the United States." Mrs. Smith's office is responsible for maintaining certain accounts of the government and issuance of the daily statement of the United States Treasury, showing deposits and withdrawals of government funds. All government checks are drawn on the Treasurer. She is also Treasurer of the Board of Trustees of the Postal Savings System. Her office is under the Fiscal Service of the department since the President's reorganization of the department in June, 1940.

Mrs. Smith's signature appears on all paper money issued by the government, along with that of the Secretary of the Treasury. She succeeded a woman, Mrs. Ivy Baker Priest, in office. She has had wide political, civic and business experience, and was at one time a reporter for the San Rafael (California) *Independent Journal*. She was a member of Governor Edmund Brown's Business Advisory Committee in California, a former National Democratic Committeewoman, and was active in most California statewide campaigns since 1954. She is a graduate of the University of Michigan where she received a degree in Far Eastern Civilizations.

The first bills bearing the signatures of Secretary Dillon and Mrs. Smith rolled off the presses January 24, 1961. The two officials watched uncut sheets of thirty-two one-dollar bills come off the presses at the Bureau of Engraving that day. The bills started with the serial number A00000001A and the series year designation was 1957A. Incidentally, the series year changes only when significant changes are made in the design of a bill. The '57 series was the result of the addition of the motto, *In God We Trust*, to the reverse side of the dollar bill and carried the signatures of former Secretary Robert B. Anderson and Treasurer Ivy Baker Priest.

Mrs. Priest once used her signature on a dollar bill as identification to charge a meal at a plush Hollywood restaurant.

Under Secretary of the Treasury Henry H. Fowler

Mr. Fowler is second in command at Treasury. He has general supervision over all functions of the department and acts as Secretary of the Treasury in the absence of the Secretary.

Mr. Fowler has served as Administrator of the Defense Production Administration, the National Production Authority, and Director of the Office of Defense Mobilization—as well as having held a long list of other important government posts. In private life, he was senior member of an important Washington law firm.

Under Secretary of the Treasury for Monetary Affairs Robert V. Roosa

Mr. Roosa is responsible to the Secretary for Treasury debt management policies. A University of Michigan graduate, who holds a Ph.D. in economics, Mr. Roosa has taught at Michigan, Harvard and MIT. He has had a long and successful career in banking with the Federal Reserve Bank of New York and is the author of many erudite works on banking, credit, economics, statistics, international finance and other subjects.

Assistant Secretary of the Treasury Stanley S. Surrey

Mr. Surrey is in charge of developing tax policy for the Treasury.

A graduate of the City College of New York (Phi Beta Kappa and *magna cum laude*), Mr. Surrey took his law degree from Columbia Law School, where he edited the law review. He is the co-editor of several books on federal income taxation, and has served on U. S. tax missions to Japan, Venezuela and other countries. He is in charge of the Tax Analysis staff, the Office of Legislative Counsel and the Office of International Tax Affairs.

Assistant Secretary of the Treasury John M. Leddy

Mr. Leddy's responsibilities are concerned with international financial matters. Mr. Leddy is a former State Department colleague of Secretary Dillon's, who moved over with his chief. He advises the Secretary in the formulation and executive of policy decisions in international finance and monetary affairs. A graduate of Georgetown's Foreign Service School, he entered the government in the 1930's and culminated his work in the State Department as an assistant to the Under Secretary.

Assistant Secretary of the Treasury A. Gilmore Flues

Appointed by President Eisenhower in 1957, Mr. Flues was asked to remain in the Treasury by Secretary Dillon. His jurisdiction includes Customs, the Mint, the Narcotics Bureau, and Engraving and Printing. He also directs the Coast Guard, the Secret Service and the Office of Law Enforcement Co-ordination. A Harvard law graduate, he served in the Air Force and with the OSS during World War II.

Assistant Secretary of the Treasury William T. Heffelfinger (Fiscal)

Mr. Heffelfinger, a career official, joined the Treasury Department in August, 1917, as a messenger, and worked up the ladder in many posts. He works closely with the Under Secretary for Monetary Affairs and is responsible for the administration of Treasury financing operations. He also acts as a liaison between Treasury and other government departments with respect to their financial operations; directs the performance of the fiscal agency functions of the Federal Reserve Banks, supervises the current cash position of the Treasury, and directs the transfer of government funds between Federal Reserve Banks.

CHAPTER FIVE

Luther Hodges and the Department of Commerce

THE OFFICE——The Secretary of Commerce is the official spokesman for American business within the Cabinet—the President's principal contact with the business world. In that capacity, he is responsible for advising the President on federal policy and programs that affect the nation's business, industrial and commercial activities.

Although usually one of the least publicized of the Cabinet posts, the Secretaryship of Commerce is one of the most important of all federal posts. Few things are more important to all citizens than the state of business—whether the nation enjoys prosperity or is mired in recession or depression. Programs advocated by the Secretary of Commerce often have considerable influence on business prosperity or the lack of it.

At least two Secretaries of Commerce in the recent past, Henry A. Wallace and Sinclair Weeks, attracted great controversy. One Secretary of Commerce, Herbert Hoover, found the post a steppingstone to the White House. Secretary Hoover served from 1921 until 1928, when he was elected President.

Founded in 1903 as the Department of Commerce and Labor, the department was split in two in 1913.

The Department of Commerce has a budget of about three and a half billion dollars.

Among the important bureaus of the Commerce Department are the Patent Office, the National Bureau of Standards, the Census Bureau, the Office of Business Economics, the Coast and Geodetic Survey, the Bureau of Public Roads, the Weather Bureau, the Maritime Administration, the Bureau of Foreign Commerce, and many important boards and committees. Some of these include the National Inventors' Council, the Foreign-Trade Zones Board, the St. Lawrence Seaway Development Corporation and the Office of International Trade Fairs.

A brief description of each bureau follows:

The Office of Business Economics provides basic measures of the national economy and current analysis of short-run changes in the economic situation and business outlook. It develops and analyzes the national income, balance of international payments, and many other business indicators. Such measures are essential to its job of presenting business and government with the facts required to meet the objective of expanding business and improving the economy.

Bureau of the Census: The first census was taken in 1790. Each ten years since a new census has been taken. Besides counting noses, the Census Bureau obtains a vast array of information of value to American business, compiling data on agriculture, manufacturing, trade, sales of retail stores and other material. It publishes an immensely valuable book: *The Statistical Abstract of the United States* each year. It puts out monthly, quarterly and annual reports for many industries.

Coast and Geodetic Survey: Functions of the Coast and Geodetic Survey are: (1) surveying and charting the coasts of the United States, its Territories and possessions and the printing of nautical charts to insure safe navigation; (2) hydrographic and topographic surveying of some inland waters; (3) the determination of geographic positions and elevations along the coasts and in the interior of the country, to co-ordinate coastal surveys and to provide a framework for mapping and other engineering work; (4) the study of tides and currents in order to make annual tide and current forecasts; (5) the compilation and printing of aeronautical charts for civil aviation; (6) observations of the earth's magnetism for information essential to the mariner, aviator, land surveyor, radio engineer and others; (7) seismological observations and investigations to supply data for designing structures resistant to earthquakes; and (8) gravity and astronomic observations to provide basic data for geodetic surveys and studies of the earth's crust.

Bureau of Foreign Commerce: The Bureau of Foreign Commerce promotes foreign trade, investment and travel. Its functions are carried on mainly by the Office of Economic Affairs, the Office of Trade Promotion, the Office of Export Supply and the Office of International Travel.

BFC informational services are geared to the needs of the business community. Publications include the magazine *Foreign Commerce Weekly,* which gives the latest information received from U. S. Foreign Service posts of interest to American foreign traders and investors and, in addition to

79

economic and commercial news and feature articles, carries announcements of specific opportunities for export, import and agency business, for licensing agreements, and for foreign investment.

BFC also issues numerous economic, operational and statistical reports issued by country in the *World Trade Information Service;* a series of investment guides to help businessmen survey the conditions and outlook for investing and marketing abroad; and special publications covering a wide range of information, such as *Channels for Trading Abroad, Survey of International Travel,* and the *Comprehensive Export Schedule* which contains regulations governing exports from the U.S.

From the bureau foreign traders can obtain *Trade Lists* giving the names and addresses of businessmen abroad who make, buy or sell specific commodities or operate services. And for help in selecting reliable connections, traders can get *World Trade Directory* reports on individual foreign business firms. The bureau aids American businessmen going abroad and foreign businessmen visiting the United States to establish trading relationships; informs U. S. owners of patents, trademarks and copyrights about industrial property protection abroad; and advises United States firms in connection with disputes arising from trade or investment transactions. It also carries on activities implementing the Foreign-Trade Zones Act, and administrates the Export Control Act.

The Maritime Administration and Federal Maritime Board have the vital task of promoting and maintaining an adequate merchant marine for the United States. The board administers the various shipping laws with respect to the control of rates, services, practices and agreements of common carriers by water. It grants subsidy contracts to steamship companies which agree to operate vessels on certain trade routes found essential to the nation's trade and defense. It also subsidizes the building of ships for use in U. S. foreign trade. (The subsidy payments are designed to offset lower operating and construction costs of foreign-flag shipping.)

The Maritime Administration administers subsidy agreements, maintains more than two thousand government-owned merchant ships in reserve fleets, maintains shipyards in stand-by condition, and operates the U. S. Merchant Marine Academy for the training of licensed ship's officers.

Bureau of Public Roads: The Bureau of Public Roads, created in 1893 o study road-building methods, administers federal aid to the states for highway construction, supervises road building on federal lands, and conducts research relating to highways.

The National Bureau of Standards, established by Congress in 1901, maintains the nation's standards of physical measurement, and undertakes vast and extremely important scientific research. It has sixteen divisions: electricity-electronics, optics and metrology, heat, atomic and radiation physics, chemistry, mechanics, organic and fibrous materials, metallurgy, mineral products, building technology, applied mathematics, data-processing systems, cryogenic engineering, radio propagation physics, radio propagation engineering and radio standards. It performs one of the least-known and most important of all government functions.

Patent Office: Created under a direct grant of power from the U. S. Constitution, this important agency has granted almost three million patents since 1790. It publishes the *Official Gazette* containing newly issued patents and trade-marks.

Weather Bureau: The Weather Bureau is responsible for observing, reporting and forecasting the weather for the public. Storm warnings, flood warnings, weather forecasts, and other meteorological information are made available to the general public by television, radio, telephone and newspapers. Specialized weather services required for air transportation, agriculture and shipping are also provided.

THE MAN——Secretary of Commerce Luther Hartwell Hodges, 68, is a tall, silver-haired man of commanding presence, deep blue eyes and an unfailing sense of courtesy. Listening to him speak in a quiet voice, gently tinged with a soft, Southern accent, one is struck with an apparent contrast between Mr. Hodges and some other members of the Kennedy Cabinet, who remind one of brilliant, young college professors.

By constrast, Mr. Hodges reminds one of a faintly aristocratic Southern colonel of the old school, mellowed with wisdom and experience. Unlike some of his colleagues, he almost never *seems* to be in a hurry. (This is deceptive, for Secretary Hodges yields to no one in his ability to get complex and difficult tasks done quickly.)

He is of a different generation from most of his colleagues. At 63, he is the dean of the Cabinet—whose ages averaged 47.3 years at the time of taking office. Mr. Hodges' maturity adds a balance to the Cabinet it would not otherwise have.

The Secretary of Commerce is a businessman's businessman. He rose literally from birth in a log cabin as the son of a tenant tobacco farmer to become the President's top adviser on business affairs.

By his own efforts, he educated himself, became wealthy in a brilliant and constructive business career, fought the political bosses to become a highly successful Governor of North Carolina. Then, to his own surprise, he became the second member of the Kennedy Cabinet to be selected.

Born March 9, 1898, in the bleak tobacco country of Pittsylvania County, Virginia, in a log cabin which his father built with his own hands, Mr. Hodges was the eighth of a large family of nine children.

When he was a year old, his family moved to Leaksville, North Carolina, a small, cotton mill town just south of the Virginia state line. Mr. Hodges' mother died when he was six. At twelve, his schooling was temporarily interrupted when he took a job in the cotton mill to help with the expenses of the large and struggling family.

But the desire to get an education and better himself never dimmed for Mr. Hodges. He returned to school and worked at the mill after school hours. His pay was fifty cents per day.

With less than a hundred dollars, saved painfully from his work at the mill and from peddling newspapers and magazines on railroad trains, seventeen-year-old Luther Hodges enrolled at the University of North Carolina. He worked his own way through college, waiting on tables and doing odd jobs like firing furnaces. His college career was interrupted by the outbreak of the First World War. He served briefly as an Army lieutenant, and then returned to the University of North Carolina to receive his degree.

Having worked in cotton textile mills and grown up in the industry, it was natural that young Hodges would choose to enter the textile field. He began as assistant manager in the same mill where he had once been employed as a mill hand and office boy.

Mr. Hodges' rise was steady and spectacular for the conservative textile mill industry. He became manager of the mill in his home town, and his reputation as an expert in textiles spread throughout the industry. In 1938, at 40, he became general manager in charge of manufacturing for Marshall Field and Company. (Though best known as the fabulous Chicago department store, Marshall Field is active in many enterprises and operates a system of more than thirty textile mills. Hodges was in charge of all of them.)

In 1922, the future Secretary of Commerce married pretty Martha Blakeney in Union County, North Carolina. Mrs. Hodges was a school teacher at Leaksville when they met. They have two daughters, Betsy (Mrs. D. M. Bernard, Jr.) of Anacortes, Washington; Nancy (Mrs. John C. Finlay) of Rangoon, Burma; and one son, Luther, Jr., who is now attending the Graduate School of Business Administration at Harvard University.

Luther Hodges got his first taste of government service in 1944 during the administration of Franklin Delano Roosevelt, when he was selected to head the important Textile Division of the Office of Price Administration. This was during World War II, when shortages, rationing and price ceilings plagued the industry. In 1945, he was named a consultant to Secretary of Agriculture Clinton Anderson.

In 1950, Mr. Hodges retired from private business. He spent over a year in West Germany as head of the Industry Division of the Economic Co-operation Administration, assisting General Lucius Clay, and served as consultant to the State Department in the latter months of 1951 on the International Management Conference.

The turning point in Hodges' life came in 1952. Almost "on a dare," he entered active duties. Almost totally unknown, he threw his hat into the ring as candidate for Lieutenant Governor of North Carolina—an ambitious beginning, since it was the second-highest office in the state.

"For years I'd been preaching that businessmen should get into politics," Secretary Hodges told the authors. "So, when I retired, my friends recalled to me what I'd been saying, and I entered the primary election contest for Lieutenant Governor almost on a dare."

Four candidates were running. Few, if any, professional politicians or political observers gave Hodges, the rank amateur and outsider, the remotest chance of winning. None looked for him to finish higher than fourth.

The Hodges campaign was strictly the "shoe leather" variety, he told us.

During the campaign, he made the rounds of all of North Carolina's one hundred counties. "No candidate for Lieutenant Governor in North Carolina had ever done that before," Mr. Hodges told the authors.

He recalled with a chuckle how: "One cold February day, I came to a country store in the northeast corner of the state. There were two hard-bitten farmers sitting around a potbellied stove. I told them who I was and asked them to vote for me.

"They didn't even look at me. For a long time, neither one of them said anything. Then one of them said: 'I guess we'll hafta be for you. There ain't been nobody else around!'

"I'll never forget the first political card I gave away," the Secretary of Commerce resumed with a smile. "I had breakfast at a hotel—my check came to sixty-five cents—and I was scared to death about asking people to vote for me. My hands were sweating when I handed the cashier a card that said 'Luther Hodges For Lieutenant Governor'—I almost ran out the door, but I managed to blurt out: 'I hope you'll vote for me.' "

"The cashier looked at me and smiled. 'Mister,' she said, 'I'm fer ya 'cause ya ain't in Washington or Raleigh now!'

"That was the key to the campaign, I think. People wanted a fresh approach."

All during the campaign he never made a single speech, Mr. Hodges said. But he would chat informally with people and tell them: " 'In this state, political groups with much to gain have always hand-picked the Lieutenant Governor. You ought to choose the person to fill the office with care. Someday the Lieutenant Governor may become Governor.' It hadn't happened in seventy-five years, and I don't suppose anyone ever expected that it ever would happen. But, within forty-eight hours of the time the Governor and I were inaugurated, he had a heart attack."

Hodges had no campaign manager and "didn't spend a cent for help at the polls"—usually a major item of expense with every successful politician. In spite of all his disadvantages, he won—the most stunning political upset in many decades of North Carolina political history.

Two years later, Governor William Umstead died. Luther Hodges, the novice politician, became Governor.

As Governor, the future Secretary of Commerce had a spectacular, if somewhat controversial, career. He won a nationwide reputation for two things: (1) averting racial violence in the wake of the Supreme Court's famous decision desegregating the public schools, and (2) attracting new industry to North Carolina.

North Carolina was expected to be one of the first "battlegrounds" of the South in the desegregation crisis. Agitators of both races were itching for a fight in the Southern border

84

state. Governor Hodges appointed responsible citizens to committees to ease the tensions of integration, and firmly let it be known that violence would not be tolerated. Integration proceeded quietly in North Carolina. The tragic strife of Little Rock and New Orleans was avoided.

In attracting new industry to North Carolina, Luther Hodges was successful beyond his most fervent expectations. In his last year in office alone, he traveled 75,000 miles singing the praises of the Tarheel State as a site to locate new factories. He persuaded 204 local communities to form development boards to lure new industry to the state. His aim was the "upgrading" of North Carolina industry to provide new jobs and new opportunities. Re-elected to a full term as Governor in 1956, Mr. Hodges accelerated his program of attracting new industry to the state.

According to the state's Division of Commerce and Industry, new capital expended on plants and expansion totaled more than one *billion*, one hundred and fifty million dollars! This created 318,233 new jobs and added $431,539,000 to the state's annual payroll. Over 2,300 new plants were built, according to the state's figures.

A highlight of Hodges' career as Governor of North Carolina was the enactment of the first state minimum-wage law passed in the South—seventy-five cents per hour for work done inside the state. Despite this, he had substantial opposition from organized labor and was denounced by Union Leader James B. Carey for having an "illiberal and reactionary" labor record. The blast from the fiery Mr. Carey obviously did Secretary Hodges far more good than harm with his business "constituents."

Mr. Hodges' selection as Secretary of Commerce came as a considerable surprise to many observers—including himself, he declares. At the Democratic National Convention of 1960, Governor Hodges supported Lyndon Johnson of Texas. But when Senator Kennedy was nominated, he vigorously supported the Massachusetts lawmaker. As an influential businessman, he was named to head the National Businessmen for Kennedy Committee.

"But nothing was ever said at any time during the campaign about an office in the new administration," Mr. Hodges said, "and I planned to retire after leaving the Governor's office. My wife and I bought a home in Chapel Hill, and we were planning to take it easy."

85

But, on December 2, Mr. Hodges received a telephone call from the President-Elect, asking him to come to Palm Beach and see him. The following day the soft-spoken North Carolinian was introduced to a crowd of eager reporters as the second member of the Kennedy Cabinet.

As Secretary of Commerce, Luther Hodges has begun a notable crusade to "get America's industrial machine strengthened, modernized, and up to date."

If he succeeds, the results will be far-reaching.

"The biggest danger to American trade," he told the writers, "is that in too many areas we're priced too high." One of his first steps was to "challenge" both business and labor to eliminate feather-bedding and other restrictive and wasteful practices. "We're priced out of the market in soft goods and component parts, for example," he said.

"Some of our friends and allies have come out of the ruins of World War II to build an industrial plant that is more modern than ours," he said. "American business ought to spend seventy-five to ninety billion dollars to modernize its industrial plant." This, he believes, would create a great number of jobs and would enable the United States to compete effectively with nations having wage scales lower than ours.

To release the funds to undertake such a tremendous rebuilding job, the Secretary of Commerce advocates liberalizing the nation's tax depreciation laws to enable companies to finance the purchase of new and better machinery. Present tax laws, which require depreciation over a period of many years, sometimes "freeze" obsolete equipment in use in American plants.

"We must make our tax laws the instrument of incentive rather than an alibi for indifference." Foreign competitors, he points out, paying cheaper wages and using newer, more efficient productive machinery, are underselling American companies in the world market, in some important industries.

A persuasive man, with a pleasant, courteous and highly effective manner of bringing others around to his way of thinking, Luther Hodges is regarded by his business friends as a "supersalesman." He accepts this as a compliment. At one of his press conferences, entirely unnoticed amid announcements of roads, foreign trade, anti-recession programs and the like, he made a few, informal comments which give the flavor of the Secretary's personality and beliefs.

"Too many Americans," he remarked, "have lost the art of doing business pleasantly. Try to go to a railroad station, for instance, and get some courteous treatment . . . and the airlines are getting just as bad. When you go to a hotel the desk clerk acts like he's doing you a big favor to give you a room . . . even if he's got a lot of rooms. America needs to do some selling if we're going to regain our position in the world market."

When increased agricultural price supports for cotton were announced, Secretary Hodges commented, in a wryly humorous vein, "the situation gets worser and worser. We are putting a basic American industry necessary to the national defense at an impossible price disadvantage," he said frankly, in a rare example of Washington straight talk on a highly controversial subject.

The industry referred to was the hard-hit American textile industry, already badly bruised by price competition from nations where wage scales are only one-fifth of American wage scales. It is a situation where three departments of government become involved in the affairs of a single industry. The Commerce Department is concerned because it affects business, the State Department because it concerns international affairs involving several friendly nations with whom the United States has alliances, the Agriculture Department because of the impact upon growers of U. S. cotton. Under the Secretary's leadership, a program to assist the textile industry has been announced.

"Basically, America can meet competition from other nations," Hodges declares. "But we *must* get our industrial machine more modern, more competitive—especially cost-wise—and we must get down to doing some real selling rather than coasting.

"When I leave the Department of Commerce," Mr. Hodges told the writers, "I'd like to have it said that I and my associates 'revitalized' the department—that we, if you please, 'merchandised' it to the American people. That we have a Census Bureau that works more efficiently and a Patent Office that is more efficient and more up to date and which causes the ingeniousness of the American people to invent more things . . . a Bureau of Standards as modern as tomorrow. And that goes for the domestic field, too. American business and the American people need better tools with which to work, from the Commerce Department. We must be in a stronger position to compete with foreign countries. Frankly, in some ways, they are more modern than we are."

Secretary Hodges' appointment is regarded as extending the

olive branch to the business community by the Kennedy Administration—to allay fears of excessive federal spending.

Under Secretary of Commerce Edward Gudeman

A graduate of Harvard, Mr. Gudeman has been a businessman all his life. He joined the staff of Sears, Roebuck and Company as a trainee at the completion of his college work in 1927. In 1952, he was appointed Vice President of Merchandising, a position he held until he resigned in 1959. In December, 1959, Mr. Gudeman became a consultant and Director of the Brunswick Corporation and a director of several manufacturing and investment firms.

Under Secretary of Commerce Clarence D. Martin, Jr. (Transportation)

Mr. Martin is a graduate of Harvard College. He also took a year of study at the University of Washington Law School before entering business life. As a graduate of the Harvard ROTC he was called up for service in the Navy in May, 1941, and spent five years on active duty. He was a naval aviator, a patrol plane commander, and finally Commanding Officer of the U. S. Naval Air Facility, Middle River, Maryland. Mr. Martin's business career was in fields of real estate, manufacturing, and in the hardware wholesale and raw materials business.

Assistant Secretary Rowland Burnstan (International Affairs)

Mr. Burnstan supervises the Bureau of Foreign Commerce and the Office of International Trade Fairs.

Mr. Burnstan is a graduate of Lafayette College, Pennsylvania, and holds a Ph.D. degree from Columbia University. He has been both a businessman and a college professor. He was a lecturer in economics at the University of Chicago and at Carlton College in Northfield, Minnesota, where he was the chairman of the department of economics.

Assistant Secretary Hickman Price, Jr. (Domestic Affairs)

Mr. Price, a Columbia University graduate, has a long record of public service and of private business activity. He served with the Foreign Economic Administration on various economic missions, particularly in Africa and the Near East. He has been an executive of the Graham-Paige Motor Corporation of Detroit and both Treasurer and Executive Vice President of the Kaiser-Frazer Export Corporation.

He was also President of Willys-Overland Export Corporation, and most recently the Executive Vice President and Director of Mercedes-Benz do Brazil at Sao Paulo.

CHAPTER SIX

Stewart Udall and the Interior Department

THE OFFICE——The Secretary of the Interior is not usually well known in the East, but in the Western half of the United States he is often the second most important man in government, next to the President.

For one thing, the Interior Department controls or owns vast public lands, amounting to more than one-third of the entire area of the United States! In some Western states, more land is owned or controlled by the Interior Department than is owned by private citizens. The Interior Department has more than fifty thousand employees, and its annual budget is in excess of $800 million.

Consider the following:

• The Department of the Interior encompasses activities that affect the lives of all Americans, directly or indirectly, every day in the year.

• The Department of the Interior manages 600 milllion acres of land in the United States and the Territories, and has secondary or mineral-leasing responsibilities for an additional 280 million acres. It administers also the federal areas of the Outer Continental Shelf.

• It markets electric power from plants with an installed capacity of about eight million kilowatts.

• It provides irrigation water for more than seven million acres of agricultural land.

• It provides for the welfare of about 400,000 Indians.

• It increases the national minerals potential by developing and improving mining and promoting conservation of mineral resources.

• It administers almost two hundred national parks and

89

monuments, three Territories, one commonwealth, certain island possessions and ninety-six Trust Territory island units.

• It promotes conservation and development of vital fish and wildlife resources and protects these resources from unnecessary depletion.

• It surveys water and mineral resources with an eye to the future.

• It provides for the geologic and topographic mapping of the nation.

• The Interior Department also promotes mine safety; conserves vital scenic, historic, rangeland and park areas; irrigates reclaimed arid lands of the West; manages helium plants and hydroelectric power systems; and conducts geologic research and surveys. It also does research in saline water conversion.

• The Department is further responsible for the welfare of about 150,000 people in the Territories and island possessions, and in the Trust Territory of the Pacific Islands. It exercises trusteeship for the well-being of about 380,000 Indians, Aleuts and Eskimos along with resource management on about 57 million acres of Indian-owned lands.

Created by Act of Congress signed on March 3, 1849, the Department of the Interior has been called the "mother of departments" since three federal departments of Cabinet status—Agriculture, Commerce and Labor—evolved from activities once vested in the Department of the Interior. It has been described also as a "Department of the West" because the first half-century of the department's existence was devoted principally to opening up the great Western regions of the United States to settlement and development.

The Interior Department has four operating Divisions:

1. *Fish And Wildlife,* which has a Bureau of Sport Fisheries and Wildlife and a Bureau of Commercial Fisheries.
2. *Public Land Management,* which includes the Bureau of Land Management, the National Park Service, the Bureau of Indian Affairs, the Alaska Railroad and the Office of Territories.
3. *Mineral Resources* exercises tremendous power over the mining and oil industries. Included in this bureau are the Geological Survey, the Bureau of Mines, Oil Import Administration, the Office of Minerals Ex-

ploration, the Office of Minerals Mobilization, the Office of Oil and Gas, the Office of Coal Research and the Office of Geography, which, interestingly enough, has the task of standardizing geographic names in textbooks and on maps.

4. *Water And Power Development* contains the Bureau of Reclamation, which has charge of the planning and development of nearly eight million acres of arid lands in seventeen Western states, and is concerned with the generation, transmission and sale of vast amounts of public power. The Office of Saline Water may some day revolutionize life as we know it. If large-scale, inexpensive ways can be found to take the salt and minerals out of salt and brackish waters, hundreds of thousands of square miles of arid and almost worthless desert lands on this earth could be made to bloom like a garden. Mankind could enjoy a higher standard of living than it has ever known. The Bonneville Power Administration, the Southern Power Administration, and the Southeastern Power Administration are agencies which market vast blocks of public power created at various water conservation projects throughout the United States.

The Interior Department also has an Administrative Assistant Secretary, who handles such housekeeping matters as finance, budgeting and personnel.

THE MAN——The vast Interior empire is presided over by an energetic, young (40 when he was appointed) ex-athlete and ex-Congressman from Arizona named Stewart Udall. During his college career at the University of Arizona, Mr. Udall, even at the "elderly" age of 28 (his college career was interrupted by several years of service in the Army Air Force during World War II as an enlisted gunner on a B-24 bomber in the Mediterranean theater), Udall was good enough to make the All-Conference basketball team and played on the first University of Arizona team ever to be invited to Madison Square Garden's Invitational Tourney.

Even today, Secretary Udall has the energetic look of an athlete. He doesn't smoke or drink. Wearing his dark hair close-cropped in a short crew cut, and possessing an effervescent and enthusiastic personality, Mr. Udall might be mistaken for a high school basketball coach about to give his team a pep talk. He is five feet eleven inches tall and weighs a trim 175 pounds.

Like the other members of the Kennedy Cabinet, Mr. Udall is able, tough and shrewd. Although obviously highly intelligent, he does not have the college-professorish look of some of the others in the Cabinet.

"I'm not the Phi Beta Kappa type," Mr. Udall modestly told the writers. "You might put in your book," he added, "that my selection to the Cabinet shows there's hope for the small-town boys. I'm really from out in the sticks. I didn't make my way up from dire poverty like Art Goldberg [Labor Department Secretary] or Abe Ribicoff [Health, Education, and Welfare Secretary], but until I was twelve years old, I never left my home town of St. Johns, Arizona. Even when my family went to the Olympic Games in Los Angeles in 1932, I didn't go with them, much as I wanted to, because I didn't think I'd like a big city like Los Angeles."

Stewart Udall's boyhood was spent on a farm. "My father felt that the best place to teach children to work was on a farm," he says.

Then he attended Eastern Arizona Junior College and obtained his law degree from the University of Arizona. He practiced law in Tucson with his brother, Morris, until elected to Congress in 1954 as Representative of Arizona's Second District, which includes the whole state except Phoenix.

The 34-year-old lawmaker quickly began to make his presence felt. He became a leader in the bloc of young, liberal Democrats in the House of Representatives and was even so bold as to attack that congressional Holy of Holies, the seniority system.

Under this system, the Congressman with the longest period in office automatically becomes chairman of each committee, no matter how ill-qualified, cantankerous and obstructionist he may be. (This is roughly as intelligent as having an iron-clad rule in every company that the employee with the longest period of service automatically becomes president, no matter what his qualifications—or lack of them—might be.)

Stewart Udall tried to bring about a change in the system. He was one of the few young and vigorous Congressmen who had the courage to do so—since to make the attempt automatically meant alienating the powerful heads of powerful committees who do not like the idea of losing their posts, no matter how ill-qualified they may be.

Mr. Udall said he regarded his "most creative" work in Congress his efforts toward committee reform. The seniority system has some "very serious disadvantages," he told the writers. "It doesn't let the cream come to the top." As a U. S. Representative, Udall served on the Interior Committee and on the Education and Labor Committee. He was popular with his colleagues despite his heretical thoughts about the tradition-hallowed seniority system.

One of his last fights in Congress found him on the side of Senator John Kennedy of Massachusetts, fighting for a "moderate" labor bill in 1959. He was one of five members of the House Labor Committee who stood for this effort. They took a fierce buffeting from advocates of both a stronger and a weaker bill and were dubbed the "Fearless Five." Udall also led the House floor fight for his bill, the one advocated by Senator Kennedy.

The Interior Secretary remarked that he regarded this as his "toughest" fight on Capitol Hill. "Our bill didn't pass," he said. "But the final bill was closer to ours than to any of the other bills."

By tradition, the Interior Secretaryship is usually held by a Westerner. Udall fits well into this pattern. St. Johns, Arizona, where he was born, was founded by his grandfather, David King Udall, in 1880. His great-grandfather, Jacob Hamblin, is widely known in Western history as "The Mormon Leatherstocking," who made the perilous trip west in a covered wagon and helped to pioneer the Utah territory, where the family lived before moving to Arizona. Mr. Udall's father, the late Levi S. Udall, was Chief Justice of the Arizona Supreme Court at the time of his death.

"There are so many Udalls in Arizona," grins the Secretary, "and so many of 'em are active in politics that it sometimes causes a problem in the courts. Court schedules often have to be juggled because an attorney named Udall is scheduled to argue a case in front of a judge named Udall. My uncle, Jesse Udall, for instance, was on the ballot with me when I was running for Congress, only he was a Republican running for the State Supreme Court. He won." Another uncle, Don Udall, was elected Judge of the Navajo County Superior Court in the same election.

The Secretary of the Interior estimates that there are more than three hundred Udalls in Arizona. They have been elected to more public offices than any other family in the state, he believes—about half Democrats and half Republicans.

93

The Secretary of the Interior was an early "Kennedy-for-President" backer, supporting the Massachusetts Senator for Vice President against Estes Kefauver at the 1956 Democratic National Convention. In 1960, he swung the Arizona delegation into the Kennedy camp at Los Angeles. Udall is the first person from Arizona ever to be appointed to a Cabinet post. The whole state, Republicans and Democrats alike, recently celebrated with a mammoth Stewart Udall Day. Even Republican Senator Barry Goldwater issued a statement, lauding his appointment.

The Interior Secretary recalled the brief, bipartisan amity with a smile. "We have very spirited politics out in Arizona," he said with a grin. "Shortly before my appointment, I was running for re-election to Congress. And certain Republican newspapers lambasted me almost every day during the campaign. Then my appointment as Secretary of the Interior was announced, and I guess state pride got the best of 'em. I got a call from a friend. 'Stew,' he said. 'Get hold of yourself and get ready for a shock. The Phoenix newspapers have just decided that you're a great man!'"

Unlike some members of the Cabinet who shun politics, Udall loves the conflict of the political fray and is skilled in the infighting of partisan politics.

Since politics is an indispensable part of the American governmental system ("From controversy comes progress," are Secretary Udall's words), this makes him a more, rather than a less, valuable member of the Kennedy Cabinet. Udall is no sitting duck for the partisan criticism that is part of every Cabinet member's life. When an opposition spokesman takes a pot shot at Udall, he can count on getting a verbal kick in the pants right back.

At his first press conference, for instance, a reporter asked him to comment on a "tough" question—the charge by House Republican leader Charles W. Halleck of Indiana that he had committed an "impropriety" in calling members of Congress and "twisting their arms" to vote for the highly controversial resolution to increase the membership of the House Rules Committee.

Rules Committee reform was an early key issue of the Kennedy Administration. The conservative Rules Committee could—and often did—bottleneck legislation it disliked by refusing to permit it to come to the floor of the House of Representatives for a vote. The "reform" issue (adding two

94

liberal members to the conservative committee) narrowly passed by a five-vote margin.

With a broad smile, Udall cheerily admitted making calls to members of Congress in favor of the measure. It was "all part of the game" of national politics, he reminded reporters. "How well did you do?" one reporter asked. "I got a result or two," Udall grinned, obviously pleased. He denied that he had threatened any Congressman with the loss of Interior Department projects in his district if he didn't vote "right." But, as he himself had reminded reporters, "one-quarter of all the bills that pass Congress concern the Department of the Interior." Udall's calls to wavering Congressmen may have saved the entire Kennedy legislative program.

Critical comments by GOP Leader Halleck bothered Secretary Udall not at all. "I'm afraid," he said blithely, a gleeful smile on his face, "that Charley Halleck doesn't like it when others play the game the way he does. Charley always calls himself a 'gut fighter' who 'plays the game of politics up to the hilt.' Obviously, he doesn't like it when others play the game the same way."

On another occasion, Udall declared that Senator Francis Case of South Dakota "should be ashamed of himself for unloosing a mishmash of innuendoes which represent a sideswiping attack on my character."

The Senator had made a Senate speech in which he said Secretary Udall had given the impression that there was a link between which congressional districts got federal projects and how members voted in the Rules Committee struggle.

Denying that projects were discussed or that anything "improper" was mentioned in his calls to Congressmen, Udall declared: "I receive a daily average of fifteen or twenty calls from Senators and Representatives. Surely Senator Case does not contend that members of the Cabinet should not initiate conversations with members of Congress."

Secretary Udall's second press conference found him getting off what was described by the Washington *Daily News* as a "quick kick" at his fellow Arizonan, Senator Barry Goldwater. The Senator had charged that Udall's Interior Department appointments were "a cold-blooded patronage grab."

The Interior Secretary announced to the assembled press that he was "bored" by such "tirades." But, he added philosophically, "this is Lincoln's Birthday week, so I guess we have to brace ourselves for the Republican onslaught. Let the welkin ring."

On the serious side, Secretary Udall announced as one of his first acts an important change in policy regarding the management of the vast public lands.

"We are taking what we regard as a rather bold step," he said. "As a result of outmoded laws . . . the current process of applying for public land is outmoded and wasteful of public funds . . . it is open to abuse by unethical speculators and promoters. As a result, I am ordering an eighteen-month moratorium on petitions for the use of public land."

This prompted an irate reply. Four Republican United States Senators—Gordon Allot of Colorado, Wallace Bennett of Utah, Henry Dworshak of Idaho, and Barry Goldwater of Arizona—sent a red-hot letter to Secretary Udall (which they thoughtfully released to the press prior to mailing it to him— a fairly standard practice in this type of operation by the "out" political party). In the letter, the Secretary was "urged" to "withdraw" his "hasty" and "ill-advised" order.

Udall responded with an equally red-hot letter (thoughtfully releasing it at his press conference prior to mailing it to the Senators—tit for tat).

In an accompanying press release, the situation was described (in part) as follows:

The Secretary's letter rejects the Senators' request that the February 14 order be reconsidered or amended, and denies any intention to "freeze" public land programs. "The moratorium will have exactly the opposite effect," the Secretary said, "it will allow the Department to unfreeze public land programs that have been in a deep freeze for many years. The Department will substitute orderly business-like operations for the frozen morass of backlogs and rejected applications."

Udall is a fighter. And it's just as well for him and his party that he is. Life can be very miserable indeed for any Secretary of the Interior who can't fight back and effectively defend his policies.

There is tremendous "built-in" controversy at Interior. Financial empires are affected by decisions of the Secretary. Natural gas, oil, coal, electric power, the use or non-use of public lands—these and other resources are affected by what he does or does not do. If he sides with public power advocates, for instance (as Udall does), the sharp knives of the private power industry are honed for him. If he sides with private power (as did former Interior Secretary Douglas McKay), the highly vocal advocates of public power will be out for his scalp.

Udall's vigor has already caused some newsmen and other long-time Interior observers to pay him the great compliment of comparing him with Harold L. Ickes.

Mr. Ickes, who held office as Secretary of the Interior longer than any other man (from 1933 to 1946 under Presidents Franklin Roosevelt and Harry Truman), was exceptionally able. His public memory, unfortunately, has been tarnished in recent years by publication of his scolding diaries, which (doubtless unintentionally) portray him in a very bad light. Nevertheless, Harold Ickes remains, in the minds of many observers, the standard by which other Secretaries of the Interior are measured. Despite an irascible disposition, a biting tongue and an inflated ego, Ickes was a brilliant man for whose contributions the United States will long have reason to be grateful.

One of the most explosive of the built-in controversies at the Interior Department is "public power vs. private power." Under the Eisenhower Administration, the emphasis was on the development of private power. One of Secretary Udall's first major acts was to reverse this, placing the emphasis on public power. The Secretary laid down a five-point power program:

1. Federal dams shall, where feasible, include facilities for generating electrical power.
2. Preference in power sales shall be given to public agencies and co-operatives.
3. Power disposal shall be for the particular benefit of domestic and rural consumers.
4. Power shall be sold at the lowest possible rates consistent with sound business principles.
5. Power disposal shall be such as to encourage widespread use and to prevent monopolization.

"The Eisenhower Administration regarded public power as a necessary evil," he said. "We regard it as a necessary good."

Despite an occasional hassle with a GOP Congressman or Senator, it would be a mistake to assume that Secretary Udall is not popular on Capitol Hill. He is. Congressmen admire a man, even of the other party, who can take care of himself in a political scrap. They, too, regard it as "part of the game."

Furthermore, Secretary Udall's subtle, but carefully nurtured "small-town boy" approach is well received. Most Congressmen and Senators are small-town boys themselves. The types they particularly don't care for are city slickers who might be trying to put something over on them.

It would be a mistake, furthermore, in appraising Mr. Udall, to take the Secretary's modest remarks about his bucolic background at face value. He is a pretty sharp article indeed. He regularly reads the London *Economist* and contributes articles on government to such intelligent publications as the *New York Times Magazine.*

Udall's candor and informality have quickly made him a favorite with the press. At one of his press conferences, a sort of "old home week" (Udall's words) was held. Mrs. Udall presided, serving doughnuts, sweet rolls and coffee to the press. Special guests were Mrs. Harold Ickes, widow of the former Secretary, and Mrs. Oscar Chapman, the wife of another former Secretary. The occasion was the unveiling of magnificent color photographs showing the natural beauties of the State of Arizona.

"Now," beamed the Secretary at the hundred or so surprised and pleased reporters, "we hope there will be no—as the British say—'nasty questions.' "

Udall is very much of a family man and a vigorous advocate of "the strenuous life." Hiking, swimming, fishing, riding and camping are hobbies of the Udall family. The Interior Secretary is married to the former Ermalee Webb of Mesa, Arizona. The Udalls have six children: Tom, Scott, Lynn, Lori, Dennis and James.

Mrs. Udall is blond, pert, pretty and a Washington favorite. Despite being the mother of six lively youngsters, she manages to look a full decade younger than her years. "I keep up with what Stewart is doing by going through his brief case at night," she told the writers with a twinkle in her eye.

On his desk, Secretary Udall keeps a picture of which he is particularly proud. "I took it myself," he said as he displayed it. It was of the great poet, Robert Frost, and Udall's then four-year-old son Dennis. Poet Frost and Udall became friends when Mr. Frost was in residence as a poetry consultant at the Library of Congress.

"My overriding ambition is to be as good a conservationist as Teddy Roosevelt," Secretary Udall told the authors. "He was always my hero. Actually, I think one could call the Department of the Interior the Department of the Future. After all, we are concerned with how the face of the nation will look physically. Too often in the past basic decisions have

98

been made by default. I think they should be made consciously . . . and I will try to do so."

Under Secretary of the Department of the Interior James K. Carr

A conservationist and champion of water resource development, Mr. Carr once served as the engineering consultant to the U. S. House of Representatives Committee on Interior and Insular Affairs. Under Secretary Carr serves the Department as Overseer for Secretary Udall. He is no newcomer to Interior. While in college, he was given a job with a survey crew of the U. S. Geological Survey Office of the department on Mount Lassen, California. He was Chairman of the California Water Commission prior to returning to Interior as second in command.

Assistant Secretary John M. Kelly (Mineral Resources) was born in Massachusetts, but is a New Mexican by adoption. Since his graduation from the New Mexico School of Mines, Mr. Kelly's work has been mainly in the field of petroleum conservation. He served as a geologist in his state, has been Executive Director and prime organizer of the New Mexico Oil Conservation Commission, and has served as Director of the New Mexico Bureau of Mines and Mineral Research.

Assistant Secretary Frank Briggs (Fish and Wildlife) is from Missouri. Mr. Briggs has been a long-time member of the Missouri Conservation Commission, of which he served as chairman four times. His duties are concerned with long-range efforts to preserve and expand the nation's fish and wildlife resources. Co-operative efforts of the department with state agencies and facilities acts to improve fishing, both as an industry and as a recreational activity.

A former newspaperman and publisher, he was once appointed to the United States Senate to fill the unexpired term of former President Truman when the latter left the Senate to become Vice President of the United States.

Assistant Secretary John A. Carver (Public Land Management) is from Boise, Idaho. His main supervisory activities are in the Bureau of Land Management, the Bureau of Indian Affairs, the National Park Service, the Office of the Territories, and in the operation of the Alaska Railroad. The

99

Bureau of Indian Affairs works to help the more than 400,000 Indian peoples of the country adjust to changing times.

There are, for example, more than 350 separate treaties with the Indians and several thousand laws governing the relationship between the federal government and the Indian tribes throughout the nation. The administration of all the national parks, monuments and historical areas of the country are also centered in this office.

Assistant Secretary Kenneth Holum (Water and Power) has been a leader in Rural Electrification Association activities in South Dakota. He has been a member of the South Dakota Legislature, a member of the Missouri Basin Survey Commission of former President Truman, an officer of several electrical co-operatives, Supervisor of the South Brown Soil Conservation District of his state, and Chairman of the Western States Water and Power Consumers Conference from 1956 to the present.

CHAPTER SEVEN

Arthur Goldberg and the Department of Labor

THE OFFICE——The idea of a United States Department of Labor was first proposed in 1865—the final year of the Civil War. But it was forty-eight years before the project came to final fruition. In 1884, President Chester Alan Arthur established a Bureau of Labor, but it was made part of the Interior Department. Four years later, the bureau was given independent status and was called the Department of Labor, but it had no Cabinet status. In 1903, Congress established a Department of Commerce *and* Labor. Not until 1913 did President William Howard Taft, as his last official act, sign the bill which made both the Commerce and Labor Departments separate departments of the executive branch.

The law creating the Labor Department set as its purpose: "to foster, promote and develop the welfare of the wage earners of the United States, to improve their working con-

100

ditions, and to advance their opportunities for profitable employment."

The department has taken this mandate to "get the most suitable job for each worker and the best worker for the job." It operates in conjunction with the states, the nationwide system of public employment offices, and the unemployment insurance program, seeks to make work-places safe and healthful, promotes workmen's compensation and rehabilitation for injured workers, collects and publishes data on union agreements which might set a pattern for working out labor differences; enforces federal legislation affecting working conditions and labor-management relations; gives technical help on worker-training programs in industry; publishes occupational and labor market information; gathers and publishes statistics and other figures relating to employment, unemployment, wages and hours of work, prices and the cost of living, labor relations and work injuries; gives special attention to older workers, handicapped workers, beginning workers, veterans and others who require assistance.

In addition to the Labor Department, other federal agencies have certain labor functions. Chief among these are the National Labor Relations Board, which administers the Labor Management Relations Act and portions of the Labor-Management Reporting and Disclosure Act of 1959; the Federal Mediation and Conciliation Service, which assists in the settlement of disputes affecting interstate commerce; and the National Mediation Board and the Railroad Retirement Board, which deal solely with problems relating to the railroad and transportation industries.

Bureaus of the Labor Department, with a brief, thumb-nail description of how they work, include:

The Bureau of Labor Statistics—is the federal government's main fact-finding agency in the field of labor economics. From an enormous variety of sources, it collects facts and figures on employment and unemployment; earnings, wages and hours; prices, the cost of living and family budgets; work injuries, productivity, occupational outlook and other subjects. BLS figures are widely used throughout business and industry for many purposes, because they have an admirable reputation for objectivity and accuracy.

The Bureau of Employment Security—operates the United States Employment Service, which in co-operation with the states, helps to place workers in jobs, gives counseling and conducts tests to determine workers' skills through a nationwide system of eighteen hundred public employment offices (these services are provided free to workers seeking jobs and to employers seeking workers); has representatives work with employers to help develop job definitions and descriptions to find the right workers for the jobs and prevent expensive labor turnover; operates the Veterans Employment Service; provides special job-finding services for the very old, the very young and the handicapped; operates a farm labor placement service for agricultural workers in connection with seasonal crops; supervises the admission of foreign workers (principally from Mexico) to help harvest seasonal farm crops.

Wage and House Public Contracts Division—administers the Fair Labor Standards Act, which provides for a minimum wage, time and a half for overtime in excess of forty hours a week, and prohibits child labor under the age of sixteen years for general employment, including farmwork during school hours, and enforces record-keeping provisions for employers.

The Division also enforces the Walsh-Healy Public Contracts Act which establishes basic labor standards for work done on government contracts over $10,000.

Bureau of Labor Standards—helps promote improved working conditions, safety standards, improved state laws for intra-state work.

Bureau of Apprenticeship and Training—promotes programs in industry to teach the complex skills needed for today's workers.

Bureau of Employees' Compensation—administers federal laws providing workmen's compensation and related benefits in connection with job-related injuries for approximately 3,500,000 employees of the federal government, longshore and harbor workers and certain reserve officers on active duty.

Women's Bureau—seeks to advance the status of women workers. Serves as the central source of information in the federal government on all aspects of their employment.

Bureau of Labor-Management Reports—administers the reporting and disclosure by labor unions, employers and others of elections, business procedures, property administered and pension funds required under the Labor Reform bill of 1959.

Office of International Labor Affairs—represents the United States in the International Labor Organization and analyzes reports on labor developments abroad.

Bureau of Veterans Re-employment Rights—assists service men and women returning to civilian life to exercise their rights to re-employment in the jobs they left to enter military service.

THE MAN——One writer described Secretary of Labor Arthur Goldberg as "the Daniel Boone of the New Frontier." Seldom, if ever, has a Cabinet officer gotten his career off to such a spectacular burst of glory as Mr. Arthur Goldberg. Within hours after the gray-haired, 52-year-old, former labor lawyer had been sworn in as the ninth man to become Secretary of Labor, he was aboard the private airplane of the President of the United States, headed for New York City to mediate the New York Harbor tugboat strike. For weeks, the strike had tied up railroad traffic to New York and was slowly throttling America's largest city.

Carefully reviewing the main points of difference in the strike, Goldberg pulled out an old envelope from his pocket and jotted down what he thought the terms of the compromise settlement should be. Fourteen hours later, after a bargaining session that lasted the entire night, the strike was settled—almost on the identical terms the canny ex-labor lawyer had foreseen. New York breathed easier when the tugboatmen went back on the job and the railroads began running again.

Other strike settlements came in rapid succession. The most important of these was the flight engineers' strike, which had America's domestic airlines tied up in the worst snarl in their history. Again, the settlement was fixed almost upon the exact terms proposed by Goldberg. These settlements underlined what insiders in the labor-management field have known for years—that the breezy, keen-witted, unpretentious Mr. Goldberg is quite possibly America's most talented peacemaker in labor disputes.

In interviewing Secretary Goldberg, the writers asked him to comment on the role of the Secretary of Labor in settling labor disputes.

Mr. Goldberg, a thin, wiry man who stands a trim five feet ten inches and weighs 155 pounds, thought for a moment before answering.

"I think," he said carefully, "that the President regards me as his chief adviser in this area, responsible for helping him or acting on his behalf in this area. We have established agencies in the government to deal with labor disputes—the National Labor Relations Board and the Federal Mediation Service.

"It certainly isn't my intention to try to displace these

103

agencies. But in matters like the airlines strike, the tugboat strike and others . . . *if* the dispute is of major importance, and has nationwide impact . . . *then,* on behalf of the President, I certainly will do everything I can to help settle it. I think the President and I see eye to eye in approaching this problem. We certainly don't intend to dictate the terms of settlement . . . but we don't intend to sit idly by and do nothing."

Secretary Goldberg's spectacular success in settling strikes carries with it a special problem. Many labor disputants are likely to be unsatisfied unless *their* dispute has been settled by a peace conference presided over by the Secretary of Labor himself. This is something Mr. Goldberg is anxious to avoid. It could embroil him in endless problems and leave him time for little else.

The writers asked Mr. Goldberg what he considered the most important problems facing him as Secretary of Labor.

Secretary Goldberg rose from the leather-covered chair near the door of his small, wood-paneled office where he had sat down informally to talk with us. He walked over to his desk. "Well, here's something that would have to rate awfully high on the list," he said, picking up what appeared to be a scroll. "It came in the mail this morning."

The scroll was a rolled-up petition addressed to Mr. Goldberg. It was from union members in a depressed area and urged him to do everything he possibly could to help get industry moving again in their area so that they would have jobs. When fully unrolled, the scroll-petition must have been twenty feet long. It was signed by hundreds of names.

"Look at this!" Secretary Goldberg pointed to one signature. "Here's a man fifty-three years old who has been with his company for thirty-four years. He's been out of work for nineteen months. Here's another—a man who has been with his company for twenty-eight years. Here's a man with nineteen years' service. All unemployed. All have been unemployed for at least a year and a half."

For a moment, Arthur Goldberg studied the petition, almost oblivious of the writers' presence. It was obvious that he was distressed and deeply moved. "Those poor people," he murmured, almost to himself. Then he turned to us with a self-conscious smile. "The unemployment situation is really heart-rending. I've seen it and I know what it is to be poor."

The Secretary of Labor carefully rolled up the scroll, placed it on his desk, and sat down in the leather-covered chair again. "That impressed me so much," he said, "that I'm going to carry it around and show it to people." (The Secretary later sent his executive assistant to Ohio to confer personally with the group who wrote him.)

Secretary Goldberg sank into the chair, threw his head back deep in thought, and intently studied the ceiling. "Doing what we can about unemployment certainly gets top priority," he said. "But there are other things that must get top priority, too. One thing about this job is the *everything* has to have top priority. Certainly another thing is working to improve the climate of labor-management negotiations. These seem to have become hardened and increasingly bitter in recent years. I hope that the Labor-Management Advisory Board will help. I regard this as extremely important.

"Another tremendous problem we must face up to and do something about is automation." The Secretary of Labor pursed his lips. "We must have automation," he said. "We need it to be competitive in international trade. We can't resist it. But we must see that human considerations are observed. We can't throw human beings upon the scrap heap."

Some measure of the seriousness of the automation and full-employment problems is given by Labor Department estimates that, by 1970, 87 million people will be in the labor market, compared with 73.5 million in 1960. As machines become more and more productive, replacing more and more human workers, finding jobs for all of these persons is going to be a tremendous problem. Incidentally, the Labor Department estimates that 1970 will see $750 billion worth of goods and services produced.

Arthur Goldberg toyed with his dark, horn-rimmed glasses, put them in his pocket, and ran a slender hand through his gray-flecked, curly hair. "The Depressed Areas Bill will help," he said. "One of my aims is to upgrade the caliber of the U. S. Employment Service and to speed up retraining programs. And, of course, we'll work closely with the Department of Health, Education, and Welfare on matters of mutual concern.

"There's one thing that would be very good for you to put in your book," Secretary of Goldberg went on. "That is a plea to young people to stay in school. The better an education you've got, the better your chances are. It's shocking how many promising youngsters drop out of high school . . . and, of course, cannot go on to college.

105

"Of course, I realize that it's a matter of economic pressure," he said. "Among lower-income families, the dropout rate increases sharply.

"I know something of the pressure on children who come from very poor families," Arthur Goldberg continued, speaking with deep feeling. "I was the only one of eight children in my family who got more than a high school education. Poor families need the money that high school and college age youngsters can earn. I worked part-time all the time I was going to school, but, even so, it was a tremendous concession on the part of my family. One of the most important things you could put in your book would be a plea for young people not to drop out of school—no matter what the sacrifice—and, no matter how tough things get, to hang on and finish high school and go to college if they possibly can."

(Department of Labor economists have carefully documented figures which show that a high school diploma is worth at least $50,000 in increased earnings over a lifetime to a student. The importance of education is further emphasized by the department's carefully calculated figures that, by 1970, 20.2 million young people will be in the labor market—skyrocketing almost 50 per cent above the 13.8 million young people in the labor market in 1960. This should point up the value—to students and parents alike—of education in the fiercely competitive world of tomorrow.)

"Two of the biggest areas we've got to do something about," Secretary Goldberg continued, "are employment opportunities for the young and the old. The age group from twenty-five to forty is okay. There are enough job opportunities for them. But workers younger than twenty-five or older than forty find job-hunting much tougher. If we could solve the school dropout problem, we'd solve part of the employment problem among younger people. That would be the ideal way."

One of Arthur Goldberg's most profound convictions—advocated long before he ever faced the possibility of becoming Secretary of Labor—was the establishment of a Labor-Management Advisory Committee. The idea has been adopted by President Kennedy.

The President has appointed seven prominent persons from labor, seven management executives, and seven "public" members. The chairmanship of the group rotates between the Secretary of Labor and the Secretary of Commerce. Goldberg became the group's first chairman.

106

In creating the group—Secretary Goldberg's brain child—the President set for it the mission of recommending ways and means of promoting harmonious labor-management relations, finding ways of raising the standard of living and increasing productivity, of exploring the benefits and problems produced by automation and technical advances, of building more markets abroad for American-made goods, and of suggesting sound price and wage policies. This is a big order, goals worth striving for.

If the Advisory Committee can help solve the "communications" problem, of letting labor and management talk with each other, it will have made an important contribution, Goldberg believes.

"I place great stock in the Labor-Management Advisory Committee. Of course, it's a slow process. It's not going to change things overnight. It will take time for the Committee to arrive at a consensus—if it does. And it will take more time for their opinions to become widely accepted. But I believe it will be a real help in improving the climate of labor-management relationships."

Secretary Goldberg is a vigorous advocate of extending the coverage of the minimum wage laws to people not now covered, strongly opposing, for instance, an amendment which would exclude more than a million employees of retail stores working in *intra*state commerce (entirely within a single state). He has also plugged urgently for an increased minimum wage. Higher wages mean more purchasing power, he has testified before congressional committees, and this, in turn, raises the standard of living, and promotes a "vigorous economy."

Ending the recession is only the first step in meeting the long-run employment problem, the Secretary of Labor emphasizes. "We have to have seven million, three hundred thousand new jobs to reduce the unemployment rate to four per cent," he says. This will call for an increase in the amount of goods and services produced in the United States (the "gross national product") to $560 billion a year from the present $500-billion rate. Otherwise, "recovery" from the recession is likely to leave the nation with a still formidable unemployment problem. This has happened after "recovery" of the past several slumps in the business cycle, he notes.

Arthur Goldberg has an easy and informal way which puts the visitor at ease, but does not hide one of the world's sharpest minds.

107

"If you want an anecdote about me," he said, revealing by his words that he's an old hand at the writing trade (he is, having authored many articles and a significant book, *AFL-CIO, Labor United*), "I've got one. Nobody has ever used it before. It happened during the Inaugural Parade. My wife and I were riding in a big limousine and I noticed that everywhere I passed we got a tremendous cheer. I turned to my wife and said: 'I must be a popular fella.' She laughed and said: 'But listen to what else they're saying.' It turns out that they were mostly government employees and some of them were calling: 'Mr. Goldberg, we're counting on you to get us a raise.' "

The Secretary of Labor chuckled. "That was the secret of my popularity," he said with a grin.

Secretary Goldberg was born of Russian immigrant parents on Chicago's South Side, and his career is proof positive of the opportunities which America offers to young persons of ability and character. He was the youngest of eight children. His father died when Arthur was eight years old, and during all his youth he knew bitter poverty.

After graduating from Chicago's Benjamin Harrison High School, Goldberg attended the City College of Chicago and Northwestern University Law School at the same time—meanwhile working at a variety of money-making odd jobs. Despite the handicap of lack of time, he won the Charles B. Elder Award at Northwestern as the top student in his class. He was also editor of the *Illinois Law Review* during his final year at Northwestern. He won his Doctor of Jurisprudence degree in 1930.

Goldberg took—and passed—his bar examination before he reached his twenty-first birthday. A friendly Chicago judge, impressed by the serious-minded young man, waived the age requirement, and he was admitted to the bar before he legally reached his majority.

Between 1929 and 1948, he engaged in private law practice in Chicago, first with several of Chicago's leading law firms, but after 1933 under his own name.

For many years, Goldberg has been known as one of the best—if not *the* best—labor lawyers in America. The turning point in his career came in 1948, when, at the invitation of the late Philip Murray, President of the CIO, he moved to Washington to become general counsel for the CIO and the United Steelworkers.

Mr. Goldberg's skill in settling strikes comes from long experience as a negotiator in labor disputes. His ability to find common-sense compromises acceptable to both sides is legendary. This extends to little, seemingly inconsequential things involving the personal pride of the negotiators. Take the merger between the American Federation of Labor and the Congress of Industrial Organizations, for example. The merger, which took years to complete, found itself stymied at one point for lack of a suitable name. The longer the wrangle over this simple point continued, the shorter became the frayed tempers of the negotiators. Neither would yield the honor of naming the combined organization after the other group.

"Why not call it the AFL-CIO?" suggested Goldberg.

The idea was accepted.

Although Goldberg comes from a labor background, his sense of fairness has won him plaudits from those whose viewpoint differs from his. Outgoing Republican Secretary of Labor James Mitchell declared that "President Kennedy could not have made a better choice." Conservative Republican Senator Barry Goldwater of Arizona, who looks with favor upon very few persons, indeed, in the labor movement, called him "the best" of President Kennedy's Cabinet choices.

Despite his ties with labor in the past, Secretary Goldberg has pledged himself to be strictly neutral in his official duties. He challenges the common statement that the Labor Department is to be the spokesman for labor. "The Department of Labor is not a class department, and we are not a class country," he says often.

Vigorous action by the Labor Department and the White House, he believes, can prevent long-drawn-out strikes by emphasizing the "mutuality of interest" between labor, management and the public.

As a private labor attorney in 1959, Mr. Goldberg was critical of the Eisenhower Administration's "lack of aggressiveness" in seeking to settle the 116-day-long steel strike. "It is not enough for the President merely to fall back on Taft-Hartley procedures," he wrote at the time. The executive branch must "have a variety of methods" for helping to settle labor conflicts.

During World War II Mr. Goldberg served as special assistant with the rank of captain, and later major, to the Office of Strategic Services, where he acted as chief of its

Labor Division charged with organizing European labor behind enemy lines in undercover work.

"My role with the OSS has been highly exaggerated in some newspaper and magazine stories," Mr. Goldberg told the writers. "I was only an administrative officer. I don't rate any accolades. There were so many bona fide heroes in the OSS that I'm a little embarrassed to read glorified stories about what I did. I do think the work was important, however. I helped organize a division which reached Frenchmen, Dutchmen, Italians and even Germans who abhorred Nazism. These trade unionists helped gather intelligence helpful to the Allies and committed sabotage against Hitler's forces."

Arthur Goldberg holds the post of Secretary of Labor by virtue of making a personal sacrifice that seemed—to the writers—to be both shocking and unnecessary. As long-time legal counsel to the AFL-CIO, he was entitled to a pension of $20,000 for life. He voluntarily gave up his pension to avoid any appearance of "conflict of interest" between his duties as Secretary and his past duties as AFL-CIO counsel.

"Actually," he told the writers, "there really would have been no conflict of interest, since the pension was a vested right—already earned. But this is a difficult legal concept for most members of the public to understand. I felt that, under the circumstances, it was best to give it up."

The writers asked Mr. Goldberg what he thought should be done about the troublesome "conflict-of-interest" problem which, as currently interpreted, requires such costly sacrifices of successful men before they can serve in government posts.

"In my opinion," Secretary Goldberg said, "a blue-ribbon panel should be appointed to make a thorough study of the matter. A complete report should be made to Congress, which could then adopt by law guidelines which would clarify the situation. Then everyone would know where it stands."

Secretary of Labor Goldberg is an idealist. "We must be our brother's keeper," he said solemnly, peering through his dark, horn-rimmed glasses, "so that all the people may enjoy the maximum benefits this country has to offer."

Secretary Goldberg first met President Kennedy when he testified before the House Labor Committee of which Congressman Kennedy was a member.

Although Goldberg is the first to admit that foreign affairs are the "overriding issue" of our times, he also declares that "we cannot have a healthy foreign policy without a healthy domestic economy."

"America needs industrial peace to prosper and defend itself," he says.

He points out that at the time he took office as Secretary of Labor 101 out of 150 major industrial areas were in distress because of unemployment.

"This was the highest unemployment since the great depression," he said.

However hectic his public life, Arthur Goldberg's home life offers him a haven of peace and respite. His wife Dorothy (nee Kurgans) is an artist who has had many one-woman shows and is associated in the operation of a prosperous art gallery in Washington. Mrs. Goldberg is a handsome brunette, slim and always meticulously chic in appearance. She paints often in a strange abstract manner using words as well as color to express what she is trying to convey.

A recent work dedicated to the great American poet, Robert Frost, shows swirls of dramatic color with the words "lovely, dark and deep" worked into the painting. The style might be considered slightly reminiscent of Japanese paintings, which often include words of a poem in the fabric of the painting itself as part of the over-all design. It's interesting to note that she modestly considers herself a painter, reserving the term "artist" for those with enormous talent.

The Goldbergs' home is an old-fashioned and large brick house in northwest Washington. Many of Mrs. Goldberg's paintings are hung on the walls of various rooms, but their artistic taste also runs to other painters—mostly modern and abstract.

The Goldbergs have two children, a daughter, Barbara, a graduate student at the University of Chicago, and a son, Robert, who is attending Amherst.

Under Secretary of Labor W. Willard Wirtz

Under Secretary Wirtz is the second in command at the Department of Labor, with all the responsibilities for the department when Secretary Goldberg is away, as well as having general overseer responsibilities at other times.

During the war, Mr. Wirtz served as the General Counsel of the Board of Economic Welfare and as the General Counsel and public member of the War Labor Board. He was Chairman of the National Wage Stabilization Board following World War II; after his wartime services with the government, he returned to Northwestern University Law School as professor of law. He entered private law practice in 1955 with the Chicago firm of Stevenson, Rifkind and Wirtz.

Assistant Secretary of Labor James J. Reynolds

Mr. Reynolds, who has had wide experience in labor-management relations, is the Assistant Secretary in labor-management relations of the department.

After graduation from Columbia University in New York City, Mr. Reynolds went to work in Wall Street and became a member of the New York Stock Exchange in 1934. He served as an adviser to the Under Secretary of the Navy in labor-mangement problems and was discharged as a commander in 1946. After the war, President Truman appointed Reynolds to a five-year term on the National Labor Relations Board. Mr. Reynolds served as the Vice President of Manufacturing Services for ALCO Products, Inc., of Schenectady.

Assistant Secretary of Labor Jerry R. Holleman

Mr. Holleman is in charge of Manpower and Employment at the department. An electrician by trade, he rose within union ranks to become the first president of the Texas AFL-CIO. He served in World War II as a lieutenant with the Army Engineers in Italy, and in the Korean War as an Army Engineer company commander. While with the Texas unions, Holleman served on committees and special commissions for the state and federal governments, including Texas Industrial Commission, the Labor Advisory Committee on Farm Labor and' the U. S.-Mexico Trade Union Committee.

Assistant Secretary of Labor George L. P. Weaver

Mr. Weaver, who has spent his entire working life in the labor movement, after July 1 will be the Assistant Secretary in charge of International Affairs in the Department. After the merger of the AFL-CIO, he became the executive secretary of that union's Civil Rights Committee, and he has most recently served as assistant to the President of the International Union of Electrical, Radio and Machine Workers.

Mr. Weaver attended Howard University Law School and, in 1941, went to work for the Congress of Industrial Organizations as a member of the War Relief Committee. He has served on special assignment with the U. S. government and the International Confederation of Free Trade Unions.

Director of the Women's Bureau Mrs. Esther Peterson

Mrs. Peterson is in charge of formulating standards and

policies affecting one-third of the nation's present work force —women. She has been active in the labor field and in labor legislation work. She said she is "extremely interested in doing everything I can to assist women workers to have a good, productive life in the full sense." She added thoughtfully, "Many American women have achieved this, but many have not."

Mrs. Peterson has been a teacher as well as a professional working woman in the labor field—notably with the Amalgamated Clothing Workers of America. She received her first introduction to the problems of the working woman in the 1930's when she taught at the Bryn Mawr Summer School for Women Workers in Industry, a project organized by a group of university women.

"It was my first contact with the problem," Mrs. Peterson admits. "We were dealing with women who came to us right out of the factory." She also spent some time abroad when her Foreign Service husband, Oliver A. Peterson, now a labor adviser in the State Department's Bureau of African Affairs, was stationed in Sweden and Belgium. While there, she worked with the Swedish Confederation of Trade Unions and with the International Confederation of Free Trade Unions on problems of women workers in Belgium. Mrs. Peterson also helped organize, and was one of the first teachers of, the First International School for Working Women held near Paris, which was attended by women from twenty-seven different countries and dealt with the setting of standards for the employment of women.

The Director of the Women's Bureau grew up in Utah, majored in sociology at Columbia University. "Training is important," she reports, "in raising the potential of women workers. One out of every ten heads of households in the United States is a woman."

CHAPTER EIGHT

Abraham Ribicoff and the Department of Health, Education, and Welfare

THE OFFICE——The Department of Health, Education, and Welfare was established April 11, 1953, by congressional adoption of the President's Reorganization Plan No. 1 of 1953. This legislation gave departmental status to the Federal Security Agency, which was established in 1939 to administer major programs in the fields of health, education and economic security.

The department has five major units: the Public Health Service, Social Security Administration, Office of Education, Food and Drug Administration, and Office of Vocational Rehabilitation. The department also supervises Saint Elizabeth's Hospital (for the mentally ill) in the District of Columbia and assists and supervises in the conduct of the public business of three federally aided institutions: American Printing House for the Blind, Louisville, Kentucky; and Howard University and Gallaudet College (for the deaf), both in the District of Columbia.

Public Health Service—The Public Health Service, established in 1798, collaborates with the states in the control of epidemics, the sanitation of milk and water supplies, control of communicable and chronic diseases, control of water and air pollution, and other health problems.

The research arm of the Service is the National Institutes of Health in Bethesda, Maryland, where research programs are conducted in cancer, heart disease, arthritis, and rheumatism, dental diseases, mental illness and other major diseases. The Service also facilitates research through grants of funds to universities, hospitals and other research organizations throughout the nation.

The Service operates hospitals for general medical services for merchant seamen and other beneficiaries designated by Congress, as well as two hospitals for drug addicts, one at Lexington, Kentucky, and the other at Fort Worth, Texas; and the National Leprosarium at Carville, Louisiana. The

Service also administers the program of health and medical care for American Indians, and operates the foreign quarantine service.

The Hospital and Medical Facilities Survey and Construction Program, established by Congress in 1946 and expanded by the 1954 amendments, is administered by the Public Health Service. In 1956 the National Library of Medicine—formerly the Armed Forces Medical Library—became a part of the Public Health Service.

Social Security Administration—Four bureaus are included within the Social Security Administration. The Bureau of Old-Age and Survivors Insurance is responsible for administration of the nationwide system of old-age, survivors and disability insurance, which provides monthly benefits to qualified workers and self-employed persons who retire, to their dependents, to survivors of insured workers who die, to insured workers who are totally disabled and their dependents.

The Bureau of Public Assistance administers the federal aspects of the state-federal public assistance programs under which federal grants are made to states for aid to four groups of the needy—the aged, the blind, dependent children, and the permanently and totally disabled.

The Children's Bureau, created by act of Congress in 1912, has the broad duty of investigating and reporting "upon all matters pertaining to the welfare of children and child life among all classes of our people." The Bureau administers Title 5 of the Social Security Act, which authorizes grants to States to assist them in developing maternal and child health services, services for crippled children, and child welfare services.

The Bureau of Federal Credit Unions administers the Federal Credit Union Act of 1934, pertaining to the chartering, examination and supervision of federal credit unions.

Office of Education—The original function of the Office of Education in the act which established it in 1867 was the collection of statistics and facts to show the condition and progress of education in the United States. Under this function the Office collects educational statistics and other forms of information on schools and school systems, colleges, universities and libraries and makes reports and studies available to state and local educational leaders, schools, colleges and universities, libraries and the public. Other responsibilities have been added to the work of the Office. These include making grants to land-grant colleges and universities, admini-

115

stering programs of federal aid for vocational education, for co-operative educational research and federal funds appropriated for schools in federally impacted areas. It also has responsibility for programs of international teacher and educational leader exchange and training, in co-operation with the Department of State.

Food and Drug Administration—The Food and Drug Administration, established in 1906, enforces the federal laws designed to insure the purity, safety, quality and truthful labeling of foods, drugs and cosmetics, and safety information in the labeling of household chemical products. This includes regulatory control of imports as well as interstate shipments. The enforcement of certain predistribution controls, such as the testing of penicillin, is also a responsibility of the Administration. It formulates definitions and standards for foods to promote fair dealing in the interest of the consumer.

Office of Vocational Rehabilitation—The Office of Vocational Rehabilitation co-operates with the states in preparing for and restoring to useful employment disabled persons who have job handicaps resulting from illness, accident or other causes. The states actually provide the rehabilitation services. The Office of Vocational Rehabilitation establishes standards for state operations, gives technical assistance to the states, and certifies federal grants to the states in accordance with formulas set forth by Public Law 565, the Vocational Rehabilitation Amendments of 1954. Under this legislation, the federal Office provides grants for research, the expansion of rehabilitation facilities, and the extension and improvement of existing services and programs for the disabled. Both public and private nonprofit organizations may apply for research grants. The Office also administers a training program under which grants are made to educational institutions for the training of rehabilitation workers.

THE MAN——"Abe Ribicoff is a real charmer. He's the Cary Grant of politics: handsome, suave and loaded with talent. You'll enjoy meeting him," a newspaper friend told the writers.

The description is apt. Few have so dazzling a smile, so much personal warmth. Yet Secretary Ribicoff is no glad-handing politician. "Sincere" might be a one-word description of the new chief of the Department of Health, Education, and Welfare.

Secretary Ribicoff's office is large, with dull green rugs,

off-white walls, spacious windows and comfortable leather chairs and couches. Two ceramic donkeys (Democratic, naturally)—one fairly traditional, the other a bit bizarre—rest on his desk. He works sitting in a blue leather, high-backed chair he had brought to Washington from the Governor's office in Hartford, Connecticut. On its high, curved back are letters in gold—the motto of the State of Connecticut, which, in translation, says, "Who Is Transplanted Sustains."

Abraham Ribicoff is a man of many fascinating facets. One of the most interesting is the leading role he played in helping make John Fitzgerald Kennedy President.

"Mr. Secretary, weren't you the first Kennedy-for-President supporter outside the State of Massachusetts?" the writers asked.

The features of the Secretary of Health, Education, and Welfare creased into a broad smile. "No," he smiled. "That's wrong."

"Wrong?" We were startled.

Mr. Ribicoff gave a short and happy laugh. It was obviously a subject about which he liked to speak. "Actually," he said, "I believe that I was the first Kennedy-for-President supporter *anywhere*—outside the Kennedy family, of course —in Massachusetts or out of it. I met the President for the first time when I was a member of the House of Representatives from Connecticut in 1949 and he was a member from Massachusetts. I was impressed at once. . . I felt sure he was destined for greatness."

This early recognition of the Kennedy potential was remarkable. In 1949, Congressman John Fitzgerald Kennedy was a skinny, tousle-haired young man of 32, who looked at least five years younger. Yet there is no doubt that he deeply impressed Abraham Ribicoff. A year later, in 1950, Ribicoff wrote a letter to a constituent predicting that John Kennedy would be "the first Catholic President."

The incident is all the more remarkable because, at the time Secretary Ribicoff made his historic prediction, the country as a whole was hardly aware of the existence of two obscure members of the House of Representatives named Kennedy and Ribicoff.

This state of unenlightenment did not continue for long. The rise of each was sudden and spectacular. In 1952, Kennedy bucked an avalanche of Republican votes in the first Eisenhower landslide to unseat entrenched GOP Senator Henry Cabot Lodge. Two years later, Abraham Ribicoff was elected Governor of Connecticut by the razor-thin margin of 3,115 votes in the face of a Republican sweep. He was the only Connecticut Democrat to win state-wide office. In the years that followed, Abraham Ribicoff was instrumental in helping to put John F. Kennedy in the White House. In the first place, Abraham Ribicoff is a tremendous personality in his own right. It was unquestionably a strong boost to the Kennedy Presidential aspirations to have so impressive a figure as a staunch, untiring and eloquent supporter. In March, 1956, Abraham Ribicoff, then Governor of Connecticut and a political figure of national importance, was tthe keynote speaker a⁺ a Democratic convention in Worcester, Massachusetts.

"I was the first person to publicly put forward the name of John Fitzgerald Kennedy as a candidate for Vice President," Mr. Ribicoff told the writers. "It didn't receive much publicity then, but, in June, 1956, at the Governors' Conference, when I again boosted Kennedy for Vice President, it made headlines all over the country."

At the 1956 Democratic National Convention, Ribicoff served as floor manager for Kennedy's exciting bid for the Vice Presidential nomination. He made a stirring speech putting the Massachusetts Senator's name in the race, and was everywhere in the thick of the fray, buttonholing delegates and stirring up Kennedy sentiment.

As the millions who saw the frantic balloting will recall, Kennedy lost by an eyelash to Senator Estes Kefauver of Tennessee. However, as things turned out, the Kennedy defeat was the luckiest thing that could have happened to the future President. It made him an important national figure— and yet spared him from being associated with the Democratic defeat of 1956.

"Right after '56, we went to work," Secretary Ribicoff said, "and we worked hard."

After the 1960 convention, Democratic Nominee Kennedy entrusted Ribicoff with a delicate mission—acting as "peace emissary" to former President Harry S. Truman.

Prior to the convention, Mr. Truman declared that the conclave was "rigged" for Senator Kennedy, declared that Kennedy was "too young," and declined to attend. Ribicoff's job was to persuade the former President actively to support Kennedy in the campaign. Mission accomplished, Ribicoff plunged into the campaign himself. Tireless in his efforts to

118

elect Kennedy, he was in great demand all over the country as a speaker.

Mr. Ribicoff recalled to the writers an interesting remark he made to the exhausted Democratic nominee on election eve. "I told him: 'Jack, this is the last time I'll be calling you Jack. From now on, I'll be calling you Mr. President.' "

When John Kennedy was elected President of the United States, he was widely quoted: "Abe Ribicoff can have any job he wants in my administration."

Early speculation centered around the post of Attorney General for Mr. Ribicoff. But this stopped after wide circulation of a sentence attributed to Mr. Ribicoff relative to the hot issue of desegregation: "I don't think a Catholic President should have a Jewish Attorney General forcing the integration of Negroes upon white Protestants."

The former Connecticut Governor told the writers that he had supported Mr. Kennedy from "sincere conviction" and had "never at any time discussed any job with him. I wasn't really looking for any job," Mr. Ribicoff said. "My term as Governor had two more years to run, and then I planned to run for the Senate."

The post of Secretary of Health, Education, and Welfare seems made to order for Mr. Ribicoff. It fits in with his philosophy of "emphasizing the positive" in life. "Basically, this position is stimulating and positive," he told the authors. "Whatever you do is on the plus side. Everything the Secretary of Health, Education, and Welfare does is to *help* somebody. In the main, I prefer the positive aspects of government —and of life."

"What things do you most hope to accomplish during your tenure of office?" the writers asked Mr. Ribicoff.

"My main ambition is to improve the educational standards of the youth in America," he replied. "And there are other things, too: to reduce juvenile delinquency, provide adequate health care for our aging population; to reduce disease—to see if medical research can't find cures for the dread killers: heart disease, cancer and the others. Then, too, it is important to clean up our streams and rivers. . . and to free the air we breath from modern pollutions."

In quick sequence, Secretary Ribicoff discussed other matters with which his department is concerned which touch, directly or indirectly, almost every citizen of the land:

Item: Mr. Ribicoff is an ardent advocate of federal aid to

119

education and one important phase of this, he insists, is better pay for teachers. "Our most important asset is our children," he told the writers. "And our children need good teachers. Teachers are the key to all education. That's why teachers' salaries should be raised."

Item: The Secretary of Health, Education, and Welfare discounts arguments that federal aid to schools means federal control. "The states make the determination of how the funds are to be used," he said. He points out that the federal government is already deeply involved in federal aid to education through various grants—for agriculture, in federally impacted areas, and elsewhere. Present federal aid to education already amounts to $2.7 billion annually.

Item: Mr. Ribicoff is unimpressed with the argument that medical care for the aged under Social Security is "socialized medicine."

"Some opponents of the program keep referring to it as 'socialized medicine.' Actually, private physicians are in no way concerned with the program. The doctor-patient relationship is not affected. The program covers hospital costs, nursing home expenses, outpatient care and the like.

"It is only a question of time before the bill becomes law. There is a basic need of the American people not now being fulfilled."

Secretary Ribicoff's ability to reconcile persons of violently opposing viewpoints is legendary. The writers asked hm about this.

"The first thing, I think, is to realize that no one has all the answers," he said. "From experience, I know that a man may disagree with me and still be as sincere as I am. Certainly I should have a willingness to listen to him and a willingness to respect a person who disagrees. Few disagreements, I've found, are ever as complete or total as they may seem.

"A careful examination of the facts will often reveal points upon which it is possible to agree. Consequently, I have always made it a policy to have an open door. In forming committees, I've made it a policy to appoint people who may disagree—and by working together, we've often found that matters which seem insoluble are soluble."

The Secretary of Health, Education, and Welfare leaned back in his high, leather-backed chair and smiled.

"One other important lesson I've learned in life," he said, "is never to call people names. If you must disagree with

120

people—and sometimes you must—do it without becoming personal. Argue about issues rather than personalities. If you hurt someone deeply in a personal way, you can seldom overcome that.

"You'll never find anything I've ever said publicly that is critical of any person," he continued. "Even during my political campaigns, I tried to run on what I'm *for*, rather than what I'm *against*."

Mr. Ribicoff's philosophy of life makes it easy for people who disagree with him politically to be friendly with him personally. For example, Chairman Harry Byrd of the Senate Finance Committee, whose views on such key HEW matters as medical care for the aged under the Social Security program and federal aid to education are poles apart from Ribicoff's, commented approvingly: "Secretary Ribicoff is one of the ablest men appointed to the Cabinet in a long time."

Like two other members of the Cabinet, Luther Hodges of Commerce and Arthur Goldberg of Labor, Abraham Ribicoff came up the hard way. The son of poverty-stricken, Russian immigrant parents, he was brought up in New Britain, Connecticut.

He was a newsboy, hawking papers on the streets and he caddied at a local golf course. He delivered groceries, clerked in local stores, worked in a factory making zippers. He went to college for a year, but financial problems forced him to drop out. Then he was sent to Chicago by the zipper company as a salesman. Despite a heavy schedule, he attended classes at the University of Chicago late in the afternoon.

Working and going to school at the same time, he still found time to marry his long-time sweetheart, Ruth Siegel. Newly wed Abraham Ribicoff continued to plug away at getting an education, while Ruth Ribicoff worked as a doctor's receptionist. In 1933, Ribicoff graduated *magna cum laude* from the University of Chicago's excellent law school. He was an editor of the *Law Review,* and elected to the Order of the Coif, a national legal honor society.

At this point, Abraham Ribicoff's career reached a crossroad. He told us about it.

"I was offered two jobs," he said, "one with the Treasury Department, working on cases arising out of the government's going off the gold standard, and the other with the TVA in Knoxville. The salary offered for the Treasury post—thirty-six hundred dollars a year—was very tempting. After all, 1933 was the blackest period of the depression.

But Ribicoff didn't want to live in Washington or Knoxville. He wanted to return to where his roots were—in his native Connecticut.

After he and Ruth talked it over, the Ribicoffs went back to Hartford "to practice law for nothing."

"Sometimes you have to have the courage to turn down what seems like a good deal," Secretary Ribicoff remarked to the writers. "If you have talent and work hard, you'll succeed. You'll succeed anywhere. So my advice to young people who would like to get the most satisfaction out of life is to choose carefully where they want to live . . . and then go there. We have never regretted turning down that tempting job. If I had accepted it, the things which have happened would never have taken place. One of the most important choices young people make is to find a community they want to call home for the rest of their lives."

Brand-new Attorney-at-Law Abraham Ribicoff found his first post in the legal vineyard a humble one—a $30-a-week job searching land titles, a frequent assignment for inexperienced young lawyers. His employer was Abraham S. Bordon, whom he met through Mrs. Ribicoff's family. It wasn't long, however, before he was made a partner in the firm. Mr. Bordon, now a Justice of the Connecticut Supreme Court, summed up his opinion of Ribicoff: "To me, he was a crackerjack. He worked hard, he was willing to tackle any job. He was intelligent and efficient."

When, a few years later, Mr. Bordon was made a Superior Court Judge, he simply gave the law firm to Ribicoff. Its worth was estimated at $100,000.

"It wasn't long before I got into politics," Ribicoff told the writers. "I have always been attracted to public life."

("Politics is rich-blooded, exciting and uncertain. It is not for those who want to play life safe and cool. It takes courage to step out on the hard road of vote-getting or government service," Ribicoff has said.)

In 1938, he was elected to the state legislature from Hartford. His service was so brilliant that newspapermen covering the legislature voted him the "most outstanding" legislator in the assembly—the first time anyone could remember a first-termer winning the coveted honor. In 1940, he was re-elected to a second term.

In 1942, at 31, he was appointed Judge of the Hartford Police Court. One of his activities was serving as chairman of

122

a commission studying the relationship between alcoholism and crime. He was also chairman of the Connecticut Assembly of Municipal Court Judges.

Republican Governor James L. McConaughy appointed Ribicoff a hearing examiner for the State Interracial Commission (now the Connecticut Civil Rights Commission) in 1947.

Ribicoff's record was brilliant—but strictly local—until 1948. He was persuaded, somewhat reluctantly, to take the Democratic nomination for Connecticut's First Congressional District. The persuader was his long-time friend, John Bailey. (Mr. Bailey is now Chairman of the Democratic National Committee.)

The Ribicoff chances for election looked bleak, indeed. First, the district had long been a Republican stronghold. Second, GOP Presidential nominee Thomas E. Dewey looked like a shoo-in winner over President Harry S. Truman, and Dewey was expected to carry the GOP candidate in with him by a landslide.

"Nobody thought I had much chance," Mr. Ribicoff recalls with a grin. "On election night, nobody even bothered to make any plans for a victory celebration. It didn't look as if there were going to be any victory."

To the astonshment of Connecticut political observers, Candidate Ribicoff ran like Man O' War, swamping his Republican opponent by 25,000 votes. Mr. Ribicoff went to Congress—and the fateful meeting with John Kennedy. He was re-elected to a second term in 1950.

Ribicoff's brief four years in Congress caused considerable stir. His methods were unorthodox, but impressive. He began with the rare distinction of being assigned to the Foreign Affairs Committee, one of the choicest committees in the House, during his freshman year.

Once, press and lawmakers alike were dumfounded at being treated to a typical example of Ribicoff independence. The suave, dark-haired, Connecticut lawmaker began routinely enough—by introducing a bill for price supports for shade-grown tobacco, a major Connecticut industry. Then, after introducing the bill, Ribicoff astounded everybody by vigorously denouncing it! He called it a waste of the taxpayers' money, "a sleeper . . . designed to wreck family farms and enrich a few big corporations.

"I introduced the bill because my constituents asked me to,

123

and I felt it was my duty, but I want no doubt to exist about what I think of it."

This was astonishing enough, but the Congressman really gave politicians and press alike a jolt by denouncing a "pork barrel" (rivers and harbors) bill which would provide $32 million of federal money for a dam on the Connecticut River! For a Congressman to denounce as "a waste of money" a "pork barrel" appropriation for his own state is the rankest kind of congressional heresy.

Interestingly enough, as a member of Congress, Ribicoff voted against the creation of the Department of Health, Education, and Welfare. When Secretary-designate Ribicoff later appeared before the Senate Finance Committee for confirmation, he was gently needled by Republican Senator Carl T. Curtis of Nebraska.

"If I am not mistaken," Mr. Curtis prompted him, "did you not vote against the creation of the Department of Health, Education, and Welfare when you were a member of Congress?"

"Yes," admitted the suave and unabashed Mr. Ribicoff. "But the situation is different today. The department has been in existence for eight years and its programs are necessary."

In 1952, Ribicoff ran for the United States Senate and, for the first and only time in his career, tasted the bitterness of defeat. Although he ran 100,000 votes ahead of the Democratic ticket, he lost to Republican Prescott Bush. It was a spectacular performance of individual popularity, however, and, two years later Ribicoff was given the difficult, uphill assignment of trying to wrest the Connecticut State House from Republican control.

The 1954 gubernatorial campaign was a landmark in Connecticut political history. It looked like a tight, close race. Four days before the election, Ribicoff made a memorable speech. There were whispers—ugly whispers—directed against him about his Jewish religion, he said unsmilingly. And never had a candidate of the Jewish faith been elected Governor of Connecticut.

"But I believe in the American dream," Ribicoff said with deep emotion. "The dream that any boy, no matter what his social or economic or religious background might be, has the right to aspire to and to achieve anything open to anyone in this great country of ours.

"It is not important whether I win or lose. The important

124

thing is that Abe Ribicoff is not here to repudiate the American dream. Abe Ribicoff believes in the dream, and I know that the American dream can come true. I believe it from the bottom of my heart and your sons and daughters, too, can have the American dream come true."

In a close election, Ribicoff won—by slightly more than three thousand votes.

Ribicoff built up an astonishing record as Governor. State aid to towns and cities for education tripled; teachers' salaries were raised an average of $1,200 throughout the state; Connecticut's obsolete and wasteful system of county governments was abolished; 124 state agencies, commissions and bureaus were consolidated into 68. And the tax line was held.

One of Ribicoff's reforms was a hard-boiled campaign against speeders, drunken drivers and other traffic offenders. The Secretary of Health, Education, and Welfare told the writers about it.

"The toll in deaths and serious injuries upon American highways is appalling," he said with a slight frown. "We decided to revoke the driver's licenses of speeders, even for the first offense.

"It's an ironic thing. Some people won't slow down to save their lives—but they will slow down to save their driver's licenses." Secretary Ribicoff shook his head in wonderment at this foible of human nature.

The campaign was a success, drastically reducing traffic fatalities in Connecticut.

In 1958, Ribicoff's opponent was Fred Zeller. He won a smashing re-election victory. His plurality of 246,000 votes was the greatest ever given to any Connecticut Governor.

In 1960, after speaking in every section of the nation on behalf of John F. Kennedy, Ribicoff had the satisfaction of seeing his home state of Connecticut give the Democratic nominee a sweeping 91,000 vote majority. The Connecticut Governor was the first man called in by his old friend, the President-elect, when consultations on the Cabinet began. His was the first appointment to the Cabinet announced.

The Ribicoffs live in Georgetown. Ruth Ribicoff likes to cook, to raise house plants and do needlepoint. They rarely go out and entertain almost exclusively on a small scale, avoiding large parties as much as their position will permit. Both like the theater and to read for their own amusement.

Mrs. Ribicoff liked coming back to Washington. It gave her the chance to run her own home again. As the wife of

125

the Governor of Connecticut, she had the task of making the twenty-two-room Governor's Mansion a home. Their new house is small enough to be easily managed by the busy and popular Ruth Ribicoff, who devotes a good deal of time to civic and public activities.

Mrs. Ribicoff describes herself as an "old-fashioned" wife who thinks taking care of her husband and home is a full-time job—though she admits to enjoying politics.

The Ribicoffs, who have already celebrated their thirtieth wedding anniversary, are both extremely youthful. Both are handsome, he tall and slim, she petite and auburn-haired. They have two children. Their son, Peter, is a teacher in an Alameda, California, high school, and their daughter, Jane, attends Pine Manor Junior College, Wellesley, Massachusetts.

Under Secretary Ivan N. Nestingen

Under Secretary Nestingen is the administrative right arm of the Department of Health, Education, and Welfare. Under the new reorganization of HEW, he is not only second in command to Secretary Ribicoff in over-all operations, but he also directs the office of Field Administration, the Office of Defense Co-ordination and the Office of Internal Security.

Mr. Nestingen was Mayor of Madison, Wisconsin, before his appointment. He is young, 39, a graduate of the University of Wisconsin Law School, and a former member of the Wisconsin State Legislature and the Madison Common Council. His military service included duty in the South Pacific during World War II as a first lieutenant. He was an active Kennedy supporter in the decisive Wisconsin primary, and at one time was secretary of the "Joe Must Go Club" that sought to recall Wisconsin's Senator Joseph R. McCarthy.

Assistant Secretary James M. Quigley

Mr. Quigley directs the Special Staff on Aging of the department, the Congressional Liaison Office and the Office of Department Co-ordinator for International Activities. He is a graduate of Villanova University and Dickinson School of Law. He served for eighteen months in the Pacific theater of the war on a destroyer, and was in the Philippine and Okinawa campaigns and in the occupation forces in Korea and China as a naval officer in World War II. He was a Congressman for two terms from Pennsylvania and a former Deputy Attorney General of Pennsylvania.

Assistant Secretary Wilbur J. Cohen

Mr. Cohen is the Secretary's principal aide in preparing and presenting the department's legislative proposals. He also directs the Program Analysis Staff. He once served as Director of the Division of Research and Statistics of the Social Security Administration and was most recently a professor of Public Welfare Administration at the University of Michigan. He is a graduate of the University of Wisconsin. He served on the Economic Security Committee in 1934-35 that drafted the original Social Security Act, and he is the author of numerous books in the social security field.

CHAPTER NINE

Orville Freeman and the Department of Agriculture

THE OFFICE——Every job in the Cabinet is tough, but there are three Cabinet posts which are supposed to be "impossible." These are the Secretaryships of State, Defense and Agriculture. The Secretary of State must make decisions which, no matter how he chooses among the thorny alternatives presented in the conduct of foreign affairs, are bound to lose friends and alienate people. The Secretary of Defense, supervising a $45-billion empire, has a job so vast, made so incredibly complex by modern technology, that no man could possibly know everything the Secretary of Defense needs to know. But it is the Secretaryship of Agriculture, according to politicians, which is the "most impossible" post of all.

In modern times the Secretary of Agriculture has been a natural target for newspaper editors, farmers, politicians, irate taxpayers and students of government. Many people will violently disagree with the Secretary of Agriculture, no matter what he does or does not do.

The outgoing Secretary of Agriculture, Mr. Ezra Taft Benson, although a hard-working and dedicated man, was so politically radioactive that few prominent members of his own political party cared to be seen or photographed in his presence. Scores of Democratic Congressmen (and some Republicans) ignored their opponents and spent their time "running against Benson" for public office. Ever since former Secretary Henry A. Wallace was excoriated for "killing little pigs" and plowing under corn" in an attempt to control huge surpluses and maintain farm prices, the Secretary of Agriculture has had more than his share of sticks and stones thrown in his direction.

The "farm problem" was pointed out by President Kennedy in announcing the appointment of Orville Freeman as Secretary of Agriculture:

"I said on many occasions during the campaign that I considered the sharp decline in agricultural income to be the number one domestic problem that the country faces. The decline in agricultural income affects adversely not only the farm families of the United States, but it affects our entire economy. There is a close relationship between the decline of farm income and the recession of 1958 and the slowdown in the economy in 1960.

"The country cannot be prosperous unless all groups within our borders are prosperous. . . . This administration is going to work vigorously in attempting to improve the position of the American farmer."

At a time when costs and prices are rising, farm income has declined to about 75 per cent of what it was a decade ago.

However, when placed against the farm problems of America's greatest rival, the Soviet Union, American farm problems seem small, indeed. It is in agriculture that America makes its best showing in the cold war competition against Russia. Two simple statistics tell a dramatic story:

- In the United States, barely more than 7 million farm workers produce enough for our 180 million people to eat very well. . . . American farm problems are those of great surpluses.
- The Soviet Union, with five times as many agricultural workers produces barely enough to feed that country's population on a much inferior diet. Food shortages are doubtless an inhibiting factor on military adventures by the Russians.

History of the Department of Agriculture

The work of the U. S. Department of Agriculture first began in the U. S. Patent Office in 1836, when Commissioner of Patents Henry L. Ellsworth began to distribute agricultural seeds and plants to farmers. He had, however, no official power to do this. He sought to prove the need to use public

128

funds for this seed distribution and for agricultural statistics. In 1839, Congress granted the Patent Office $1,000 to be spent in the collection of statistics and for other agricultural puposes. It was the earliest authorization for agricultural expenditures from federal funds.

In 1849 the Department of the Interior was created, and the Patent Office became a part of it. This was soon followed by the establishment of an Agricultural Division in the Patent Office.

The Department of Agriculture was created by an act of Congress, which was approved by President Abraham Lincoln, May 15, 1862. Until 1889, the department was administered by a Commissioner of Agriculture. By the Act of February 9, 1889, it became the eighth Executive Department in the federal government.

The Agriculture Department has a budget of about six billion dollars and has more than seventy thousand full-time employees—widely diffused in every state in the union. In addition, the Commodity Credit Corporation has some nine billion dollars invested in farm commodities.

Until recently, the department had four operating divisions: *Federal-States Relations*, which included the agricultural conservation program service, agricultural research, farmer cooperative service, the federal extension service, the United States forest service and the soil conservation service; *Marketing and Foreign Agriculture*, which included the Agricultural Marketing Service, Commodity Exchange Authority and Foreign Agricultural Service; *Agricultural Stabilization* (the controversial section of the department), which included the Commodity Credit Corporation, Commodity Stabilization Service, Agricultural Stabilization and Conservation Committees, and the Federal Crop Insurance Corporation. The fourth agency, *Agricultural Credit Services* included the Farmer's Home Administration, the Rural Electrification Administration and the Farm Credit Administration.

The Department of Agriculture is the second largest government department, second only to the vast Defense Department. Its activities cover the whole gamut, according to a department witticism, from "agronomy to zoology."

THE MAN——Secretary Freeman is a lean, vigorous six-footer. His handshake is firm and strong, and he gives the impression that he retains much of the top physical conditioning which made him a quarterback on Minnesota's

129

Big Ten championship football team and a successful Marine combat officer. He has dark hair and eyes plus the ready smile and easy manner of the successful public figure.

Secretary Freeman is not at all apologetic about asking for a "better deal" for American farmers. "Agriculture is the number one American success story," he told the writers. "We in America work fewer hours to pay for our food and eat better than any people in the world.

"The average American citizen earns enough in one day to eat better for a week than people eat anyplace else in the world. Although we tend to hear much about farm subsidies, we sometimes forget the successes of agriculture. Since World War II, the productivity of the agricultural worker has grown three times as fast as that of the average industrial worker. One person, working on the farm, now produces enough to feed twenty-five persons. I think this is a handsome return on our agricultural investment.

"We need to take our blinders off in thinking about farm problems," he continued reflectively. "One of these blinders we might call 'subsidies.' The other is 'surpluses.' These blinders keep us from seeing the forest for the trees. The overwhelming success of American agriculture is one of the greatest sources of our national strength—but all we ever hear about agriculture is the farm problem."

Secretary Freeman advocates what he describes as the "supply management" approach to the farm surplus problem. It is summed up in this way: Short of war, farmers will not increase their incomes in the 1960's unless means can be found to eliminate excess production in agriculture. But this cannot be done unless farmers are able to manage the supplies of farm commoditites, and can come to a general agreement on how to do it. Many techniques for management are known, and some are now in use for doing this job. Some would require government action; others would be primarily producer-operated. All such programs are to be operated in the public interest. They would enable the millions of farmers to plan their combined output at the same time they plan their individual farm operations while assuring consumers of abundant food supplies at fair prices.

"While farmers receive an average eighty-one cents per hour for their labor, consumers do not ask farmers to produce for such substandard incomes. Nor do farmers ask for programs which would exact high prices from consumers. Farmers today receive only 39 cents from the consumer's food dollar. Farmers and consumers have an equal stake in sound farm programs. Each has an important interest in the prosperity of the other."

The man who now seeks to help the farmer in this manner was born in Minneapolis, but Secretary Freeman spent his summers on his grandfather's farm at Zumbrota, Minnesota. Interestingly enough, it was a whim of Grandfather Freeman which may have led to his grandson's becoming Secretary of Agriculture.

When Secretary Freeman's grandfather emigrated from Sweden to homestead a farm in Minnesota (now owned in part by the Secretary of Agriculture), his surname was Johnson. But in heavily Swedish Minnesota, the woods were full of Johnsons. Especially in the lumber camp where he worked. He decided to change his name to Freeman. Was he not, in America, truly a free man?

After the election campaign of 1960, when Orville Freeman narrowly missed being elected to an unprecedented fourth term as Governor of Minnesota, he had cause to smile wryly about his grandfather's whim. Mr. Freeman estimates that the change of name from Johnson to Freeman cost him at least fifty-thousand votes among Minnesota's huge Scandinavian population.

If even twelve-thousand of these voters had switched their ballots from his opponent to him, Orville Freeman would have been re-elected. But then, of course, (politics being what it is) he would probably not have been projected upon the national scene, in charge of what President Kennedy has called "the nation's number one domestic problem."

Secretary Freeman attended the University of Minnesota, where he was second-string quarterback on the Golden Gophers' football team and president of the All-University Council. This was during the depth of the depression, and the future member of the President's Cabinet worked at what odd jobs he could find to help pay his way. These included waiting tables, working as a busboy, serving as a janitor, carrying a hod, and working summers as a farm hand. This outside work did not prevent him from graduating with honors and winning the coveted Phi Beta Kappa key.

It was at the university that he met a man who was to have a profound effect upon his career—the future United States Senator, Hubert Humphrey.

Disillusioned by the bitter depression, Freeman and Humphrey developed a vast interest in politics. As college stu-

131

dents, they laid careful plans to do something they later accomplished as men—to unite and revitalize the embattled and strife-torn Democratic and Farmer-Labor parties.

"Senator Humphrey and I met—I hate to admit it was this long ago—in 1937 at the University of Minnesota," Mr. Freeman reminisced to the writers. "It was in a class in comparative government, I think. It may have been in American Constitutional development. Anyway, we were in a lot of classes together. We immediately became good friends. Even then, we both had a tremendous interest in politics. We used to have long discussions about how the Democratic party in Minnesota needed to be revitalized and how, when we graduated, we'd tackle the job of doing it.

"I was playing football, and he was on the debate team. He got me to come out for debate, too, and we often debated together. He was married then . . . unusual for a college student in those days . . . and I remember going over to his apartment often for coffee and waffles. Those were depression days. We both were convinced that the government could do a lot better job for the people than it was doing."

Freeman got his Bachelor's degree, and entered the University of Minnesota Law School in 1940. But long before he could complete his training, his plans were disrupted by war.

Mr. Freeman joined the Marine Corps Reserve in August, 1941, five months before Pearl Harbor. He was sent to Officer's Training at the Marine Corps's Quantico, Virginia, Training Center, and was commissioned a second lieutenant in April, 1942. He took part in several campaigns prior to a close call with death at Bougainville.

Secretary Freeman is probably best remembered by most Americans as the fiery, dark-haired, young orator who placed the name of John Fitzgerald Kennedy in nomination for President of the United States at the Democratic National Convention of 1960.

Few, if any, of the vast television audience, estimated in excess of sixty million persons, who heard the eloquent words of the then Governor of Minnesota would have suspected it, but the fact that Mr. Freeman can speak at all is something of a miracle. Only indomitable personal courage and the wonders of modern surgery and speech therapy made it possible.

During the intense, bitter fighting on Bougainville in 1943, part of his jaw was shot away by a Japanese sniper. As Com-

132

manding Officer of Company K of the Third Battalion of the Ninth Marine Corps, Lieutenant Orville Freeman was leading his men on a forty-eight-hour patrol through the jungles behind Japanese lines. In a brief, bitter firefight with a surprised Japanese patrol, a bullet smashed into his jaw, shattering the left side of his face.

In an agonized nightmare of pain, Major Freeman went into severe shock. It appeared for a time that he might die. He was eight months in the hospital. At first, he was partially paralyzed. His speech was grotesque, distorted. Only with courage and never-ending persistence did Freeman regain the ability to speak naturally.

"Sometimes, when I get overtired," he says objectively, "my speech is still a little slurred."

Discharged from the Marine Corps as a major, Freeman returned to the University of Minnesota Law School, where he obtained his degree in 1946. He is still a lieutenant colonel in the Marine Corps Reserve.

By that time, Freeman's long-time friend, Hubert Humphrey, had burst upon the Minnesota political scene with a mixture of eloquence and brashness which makes him one of the great natural political figures of our time. Mr. Humphrey could then, as now, literally talk rings around anybody.

Emitting words with the speed and impact of a submachine gun, Mr. Humphrey bedazzled the electorate of Minneapolis to win the mayoralty. Freeman came along as a key member of his team, being placed in charge of veterans' affairs and later as Chairman of the Minneapolis Civil Service Commission.

Meanwhile, Humphrey and Freeman began their work of revitalizing and rebuilding the Democratic-Farmer-Labor party in Minnesota. For years, it had been demoralized by defeat and disharmony.

By 1948, they were firmly in command. Mayor Humphrey won the Democratic Senatorial nomination, pitted against incumbent Senator Joseph Ball, a Harold Stassen protégé with an impressive reputation in Washington. Freeman served as Humphrey's campaign manager. In the general election, the Minneapolis major swamped Senator Ball.

Thereafter, the Humphrey-Freeman paths briefly parted. Humphrey went to Washington, and Freeman entered the private practice of law in Minneapolis. He re-entered politics in 1950, running for Attorney General. He was defeated. Two

133

years later, Freeman ran for Governor—and was defeated again. By 1954, he had almost made up his mind to retire as a political candidate and concentrate on law.

Urged by his friends in the surging new DFL party, Freeman reluctantly yielded to the pleas to make another race for Governor. He ran and was elected, the second youngest governor in the state's history. (Only Harold Stassen was younger.) Freeman won two other terms as governor—in 1956 and 1958. He lost, trying for a fourth term, in 1960. Shortly thereafter, President Kennedy announced his appointment as Secretary of Agriculture.

The Scripps-Howard newspapers had this to say about Secretary Freeman's appointment:

"Being Secretary of Agriculture is very much like crawling thru an old-fashioned threshing machine when it is in full operation. So whatever else may be said of Gov. Freeman, it would have to be added that he has plenty of nerve."

Some Republican opponents have criticized Secretary Freeman as "a city man" who "knows nothing about farming." They point out that he was born and reared in Minneapolis, hardly a rural area. Freeman counters by pointing to the experience he has had in dealing with farm problems while Governor of Minnesota, a leading farm state.

The Freeman approach is vastly different from that of his predecessor, Secretary Benson. Mr. Benson sought to return to the "free market." There seems no doubt that he would have discarded price supports and government controls if he could. (Congressional legislation prohibited this.) Secretary Freeman declares himself for using "the machinery of government wherever needed, unhampered by the worship of the free market or the fear of 'subsidy.' "

If the experience of his predecessors is any guide, Secretary Freeman's head will probably be bloody before his term is over, but he vows that it will remain unbowed. His Marine Corps experience has left him unflinching in the face of a fight—indubitably good training for a Secretary of Agriculture.

"In the Marines, there's an old saying that when you're halfway up a hill on a frontal charge you don't suddenly decide you should have used a flank attack. When you're in a fight, you don't back out," he says.

The years ahead will see greater use of American surplus foods as "an instrument of peace" in the underdeveloped nations of the world, Secretary Freeman told the writers. "This

134

is a program I feel very strongly about. It is not only to help the farm surplus problem that I say this. It is *morally* right that we who have an overabundance should help those who are hungry. It doesn't make sense for us to be piling huge surpluses of food on top of other huge stockpiles—while hungry people are starving elsewhere in the world.

"As so often happens in life, what is morally right is also logistically right. That is certainly true in using our surplus food to help feed hungry people."

"Some Congressmen have bitterly criticized your farm program as too extreme, Mr. Secretary," the writers said. "What would be your reply to that?"

Mr. Freeman shrugged. "I don't think it's extreme at all," he said. "It's logical and I think it makes sense. We need a new approach to the matter of farm production. What do we have now? Nine and a half billion dollars' worth of commodities stored at tremendous cost to the government . . . and a drop of farm income of 25 per cent net under the Eisenhower Administration. What we've had certainly hasn't worked. I think it's time for a new approach. The results speak for themselves. If what we've proposed doesn't work, we'll try something else."

"*Is* there as satisfactory solution to the farm problem?" the writers asked.

Secretary Freeman smiled. "Well, I'm one of those people who refuse to admit that there is a problem that doesn't have a solution," he said with confidence. "We most certainly can do better in agriculture. I have an open mind as to what means we use, but something—perhaps a combination of things—will work. I doubt we'll ever reach a time when we'll have 'solved' the farm problem. No more than we'll ever reach a time when we've 'solved' the problem of crime or of juvenile delinquency or of schools or of any of our other national problems. But we can do better, and I think we will."

"If you were to sum up your hopes for the Agriculture Department during your term as Secretary, what would be your goal?"

"A number of things would have equal priority," Mr. Freeman responded. "Perhaps it could best be stated as an abundant supply of food and fiber for the people of our country at fair prices—with a fair return to the farmer, commensurate with that earned by labor and capital in other industries."

Washington Columnist Don Maclean reports that Secretary

135

Freeman has a humorous formula for success: "The secret of a successful man is a wife who tells him what to do and a secretary who does it."

Under Secretary of Agriculture Charles C. Murphy

Mr. Murphy, 51, is former Special Counsel to President Harry Truman and the Senate Legislative Counsel. Born in North Carolina, he was educated at Duke University. He helped draft the Agricultural Adjustment Act of 1938 among the many farm bills during his eleven years as Senate Counsel. In 1947, President Truman appointed Mr. Murphy his Administrative Assistant. Later, as Special Counsel to the President, he acted as the principal staff assistant on legislation—including farm programs and legislation. During the 1960 campaign, he was a principal adviser to Senator Lyndon Johnson.

Assistant Secretary of Agriculture for Federal-State Relations Frank J. Welch

Mr. Welch is the former Dean of the College of Agriculture and Director of the Agricultural Experiment Station and Agricultural Extension Division of the University of Kentucky.

Dr. Welch, 58, was educated at the University of Mississippi, the University of Colorado and the University of Wisconsin. He has been a Director of the Tennessee Valley Authority, and during World War II was a member of the National War Labor Board.

Assistant Secretary of Agriculture for Marketing and Foreign Agriculture John P. Duncan, Jr.

Mr. Duncan, 43, was President of the Georgia Farm Bureau Federation. A graduate of Emory University, he did graduate work in agriculture at the University of Georgia. His office helps formulate and carry out policies and programs in connection with marketing, purchase, export and distribution of farm commodities. Included in these services are the country-wide market news reporting offices which provide information on supply, movement and price at specific current markets for practically all agricultural commodities. The Foreign Agricultural Service carries out extensive programs aimed at developing markets abroad for U. S. farm commodities.

Assistant Secretary of Agriculture for Agricultural Stabilization Dr. James T. Ralph

Dr. Ralph, 35, is a former Director of the California State Department of Agriculture. Under his direction, the Commodity Stabilization Service of the department is responsible for operation of (1) acreage allotments and marketing quotas, (2) the soil bank, (3) price supports, (4) disposal of govenment-owned surplus farm products, (5) the International Wheat Agreement, (6) the storage, shipping and related service activities, (7) administration of the Sugar Act, and (8) assigned mobilization planning His office also directs the activities of the Commodity Credit Corporation.

Dr. Ralph attended the Middle Tennessee State College, received his Master's degree in agricultural economics and statistics at Iowa State University and his Doctorate in agricultural economics at the Food Research Institute of Stanford University.

Director of Credit Services John A. Baker

Mr. Baker was Director of Legislative Services of the National Farmers Union. In his new post, with Assistant Secretary rank, he has general direction of the lending operations of the Farmers Home Administration and the Rural Electrification Administration.

He graduated with honors from the College of Agriculture at the University of Arkansas and received a graduate degree in agricultural economics from the University of Wisconsin.

Director of Agricultural Economics Willard W. Cochrane

Dr. Cochrane, 46, heads up the newest post having Assistant Secretarial status—that in charge of both research and statistical reporting services in agricultural economics.

Dr. Cochrane is a past President of the American Farm Economic Association and has been a consultant to the Department of Agriculture. He received his Bachelor's degree from the University of California, his Master's from Montana State College, and his Doctorate from Harvard University.

CHAPTER TEN

J. Edward Day and the Post Office Department

THE OFFICE——It has been said that the growth of the Postal Service reflects the development of the country to a greater degree than any other agency of the government. America today has the biggest mail service in the world, sending every year some 65 *billion* pieces of mail—two-thirds of the total world output of mail.

The Postal Service is a gigantic service, indeed, employing 560,000 civilians in its work. There are 37,000 post offices located across the nation. The Postal Service spends more than three and one-half billion dollars annually. It probably touches the lives of more people "more intimately and more frequently" than any other branch of the federal government. It is our greatest communications system and is regarded as the backbone of our economy by many experts. And yet this year alone its deficit is expected to soar to about $900 million.

Benjamin Franklin is considered the "Father of the Postal Service." He was Postmaster General of the American colonies under British rule from 1737 to 1774. The great philosopher and statesman is responsible for the original concept of the postal system.

The first Postmaster General of the United States, after the Constitution was adopted, was Samuel Osgood of Massachusetts, a patriot appointed by President George Washington. At that time, the Postal Service was part of the Treasury Department. The Postmaster General was raised to Cabinet rank in 1829. Benjamin Franklin, who did so much to establish a sound postal system, was appointed head of the American Postal System by the Continental Congress in 1775 at a salary of $1,000 a year. He served only a little more than a year in this post. He was dismissed by the British Crown for "sympathies with the cause of the American colonies."

The postage stamp, symbol of today's system, was inaugurated in 1847 when legislation was enacted authorizing the Postmaster General to issue stamps. The first such stamps went on sale on July 1, 1847, in New York City.

As the country grew, so grew the postal system. The first transcontinental mail reached Los Angeles in 1858, and by 1860 the fast and nostalgically glamorous mail service, the Pony Express, was begun. The delivery of the inaugural address of President Abraham Lincoln in 1861 set a speed milestone, taking seven days and seventeen hours—and seventy-five ponies—to cross the country. (The cost for Pony Express service was five dollars per half-ounce.) By October of that same year, with construction of telegraph poles across the nation, the service was discontinued.

In 1858, the letter-drop box on street corners was introduced to our citizenry. The postcard came into being in 1873 to facilitate the sending of brief messages. The rural delivery system, still expanding, was introduced in 1896. The Postal Savings system began in 1911. The parcel post system was born in 1913.

The air mail service began in 1918, when the first regular air mail route was established between New York City and Washington. The first air mail service outside the continental limits of the United States was the delivery of a letter from Washington to Victoria, British Columbia, in 1920. The first regular foreign air mail service was inaugurated in 1927 between Key West, Florida, and Havana, Cuba. As short a time ago as 1948, the first air parcel post system was born.

The Postal Service has a long history and a proud tradition beset with seemingly insoluble problems. The prices charged for postal service are set by Congress or established by the Interstate Commerce Commission. Wages paid employees are also set by Congress. The rates the Post Office must pay railroads, airlines and trucking concerns are also established by government regulatory bodies, and, to top this, the revenue the Postal Service earns goes to the United States Treasury! No wonder it has problems of deficit!

THE MAN——Postmaster General J. Edward Day is the wittiest man in Washington. The only other person in government who can compete with him in the brilliant *bon mot* or the delightful flash of humor which perfectly illustrates a point is his former law partner, Adlai Stevenson. But, since Ambassador Stevenson is at the United Nations in New York,

Postmaster General Day has the Washington field all to himself.

He has, incidentally, been described by Mr. Stevenson as " a man of great wit, humor and geniality, an incisive mind, and a great capacity for hard work."

One of Postmaster General Day's hobbies is collecting stamps. "I began when I was about ten years old," he says with a grin. "Now I'm wondering if I ought to sell it to avoid being charged with conflict of interest."

As a Vice President of the world's third largest corporation, the Prudential Insurance Company, Postmaster General Day (like several other members of the Cabinet) made a considerable financial sacrifice to accept his post in the administration. At Prudential, his reported salary was over $60,000 per year. As Postmaster General, it is $25,000.

"I don't feel like a hero about it," he told the writers earnestly. "It's a privilege to serve in the President's Cabinet."

"How has your life changed since you left private business to become Postmaster General?" Mr. Day was asked.

"Being Postmaster General is a complicated job. But, then, I've always enjoyed leading a complicated life. I was Vice President in charge of the Prudential Insurance Company's operations in the thirteen Western states. As such, I supervised 7,500 employees in 240 local offices and a billion and a half dollars' worth of investments. In my spare time, I served on about thirty different civic, community and charitable groups."

Mr. Day, a medium-sized man, sandy-haired and hazel-eyed, works in a handsome, honey-toned, wood-paneled office. His desk sits under an enormous portrait of Benjamin Franklin, almost a patron saint of the Post Office Department.

"My life has changed quite a lot since I've become Postmaster General," the Postmaster General smiled. "Take, for instance, all the 'by the way' letters I've been getting. They're pouring in by the hundreds."

"What is a 'by the way' letter?" we asked.

"It's a letter from a distant relative you can only faintly recall, or from somebody you've barely met, years ago, or a remote political acquaintance.

"A 'by the way' letter begins by calling you by your first name—'Dear Ed.' Then it congratulates you warmly, giving you a big build-up to the fast break that's to come. The pitch usually begins with the words, 'by the way.'

" 'By the way,' the letter will say, 'I have a brother Elmer

140

who would like to be Postmaster of such and such a town.' One letter came from a very distant relative I could hardly recall. He raises chickens in Florida. He told me he'd be willing to take a federal job—at good pay, naturally—provided he could stay in Florida. 'By the way' letters pour in all the time. It seems that there are lots of people who are willing to make the sacrifice of working for the federal government if it involves good pay."

Part of his troubles come from the fact that he's a "different" sort of Postmaster General, Mr. Day believes. "Thank Heaven, I don't have anything to do with getting people jobs in other federal departments," the sandy-haired Californian smiles. "But people remember Postmaster Generals like Jim Farley, who was a powerhouse in the party and who put thousands of people in government jobs. I don't get into that at all. My job is to run the Post Office Department. But the requests keep pouring in.

"One other amusing and puzzling thing keeps happening to me," the Postmaster General said good-naturedly. "At parties or social gatherings, people always seem to want to take up with me personally the matter of a letter that was delayed reaching them or a package crushed in the mails. One lady kept after me so much that I told her: 'Madam, if you will call me up next time you mail a package, I'll be glad to come behind the counter and take care of it for you myself.' I'm expecting any day now to get a call from her."

J. Edward Day was born in Jacksonville, Illinois, in 1914. His father was a surgeon in charge of his privately owned hospital. Later, his family moved to Springfield, Illinois, the state capital.

"I've always had a great sideline interest in government," Mr. Day commented. "Springfield is the heart of the Lincoln country . . . and I personally have always thought Lincoln was our most thoroughly appealing national figure. As a boy, I used to hang around the State House and listen to the talks of politics."

The future Postmaster General, like so many of his Cabinet colleagues, was brilliant in school and valedictorian of his high school class. He attended the University of Chicago, completing four years' work in three years. Then he attended Harvard Law School, where his grades were again among the highest. He was an editor of the *Harvard Law Review* and graduated *cum laude*.

141

Returning to Chicago, he joined the law firm of Sidley, Austin, Burgess and Smith. This association was a turning point in Day's life for two reasons: (1) he met his future wife, the former Mary Louise Burgess, the daughter of one of the partners of the firm ("We met on a blind date," she reports. The Postmaster General and Mrs. Day have two daughters, Geraldine and Molly, and a son, James Edward, Jr.); and (2) Mr. Day met Adlai Stevenson, also a member of the law firm, with whom he formed a lifelong friendship.

World War II interrupted Day's law career. Like many another of the New Frontiersmen, he served in the Navy. He served both in the Atlantic (on the Destroyer Escort *Fowler*) and in the South Pacific, where he was commanding officer of a sub chaser (PC 597). He was awarded The Navy Commendation Ribbon for duty in escorting gasoline tankers in the Solomons, and finished his Navy career a full lieutenant. Released from duty, he reported back to his law firm.

The next turning point in Day's career was the election of Adlai Stevenson as Governor of Illinois in 1948. Governor Stevenson persuaded Day to come along as one of his staff, and, a year later, promoted him to Insurance Commissioner of Illinois. He quickly became a recognized insurance expert and was elected Chairman of the Midwestern Zone of the National Association of Insurance Commissioners and Vice Chairman of the group's Life Insurance Committee.

He remained one of Stevenson's closest advisers.

"My wife and I have been close friends with Adlai Stevenson for more than twenty years," Postmaster General Day reminisced. "My wife often participated in official entertaining at the Governor's Mansion, and I had an office there. For a year and a half, I had most of my lunches there."

Day was an early booster of the "Draft Stevenson" movement for the Democratic Presidential nomination in 1952. However, with the Eisenhower landslide, Stevenson's Illinois administration, naturally, came to an end.

"The changeover from the Eisenhower to the Kennedy Administration established a pattern for a gentlemanly transfer," Day told us. "When I left office as Insurance Commissioner in Illinois, there was no such pattern. I never met my successor until after he was sworn in."

In 1953, Day, highly regarded in the insurance world, and author of many articles on legal and insurance subjects, joined the Prudential Insurance Company as Associate General Counsel in the company's home office at Newark, New Jersey. Business took more and politics less of his time. "In the 1956 election, I was only mildly active in politics," Mr. Day recalled. "I was chairman of the New Millburn Township, New Jersey, Volunteers for Stevenson."

In January, 1957, Day was promoted and transferred by the Prudential Insurance Company from the Newark home office to Los Angeles, as Vice President in Charge of Western Operations. Immediately, he plunged into politics in his spare time, presenting the rare spectacle of a topflight business executive espousing the Democratic party.

He supported Governor Edmund G. (Pat) Brown's election, and, on Election Day, 1958, ("Brown's election was a foregone conclusion," Day said) helped to form and became Chairman of a group known as the "Democratic Associates." It included wealthy oilman Edwin J. Pauley and Dan Kimball, wartime Secretary of the Navy, and other influential Californians.

Shortly after his election, Governor Brown made a cross-country trip, during which he visited Adlai Stevenson.

"You ought to get Ed Day in your administration," Governor Stevenson remarked to Brown. "He's a good man."

Returning to California, Governor Brown got in touch with Day, who offered to "help on the side"—as much as his duties with Prudential would permit. Governor Brown named him vice chairman of a twenty-man commission to study the metropolitan problems of California cities—a vast project. Los Angeles County alone contains no less than seventy-two cities and complicated problems of mass transportation, smog, highway congestion, and a galaxy of other urban headaches.

Day's first meeting with future President John Kennedy came as a result of his work with "Democratic Associates." The group, Day recalls, "was formed to help support good public officials"—presumably of the Democratic faith.

In April, 1959, Senator Kennedy, warming up for the Presidential primaries, made a whirlwind twenty-four-hour tour of Los Angeles, speaking before six different groups. Day met Senator Kennedy before his first speech, talked privately with him for about ten minutes, and became a Kennedy convert.

"I went with him to the other five meetings," Day said. "We became acquainted on a first-name basis, although I certainly was not one of his intimates. But, after that, each time he came to California, I saw him."

143

As a result of Day's political activity, he became a delegate to the 1960 Democratic National Convention, as an ardent Kennedy supporter. However, millions who watched the Democratic Convention on television were struck by the apparent vacillation of the California delegation, which, despite the strenuous efforts of Governor Brown to carry it entirely into the Kennedy camp, split wide-open between Kennedy and Adlai Stevenson.

"What happened?" the writers could not resist asking Mr. Day, who was on the inside during all the maneuvering.

"What most people don't realize or have forgotten," Postmaster General Day replied, "is that the California delegation was carefully chosen to represent all shades of opinion. We weren't trying to regiment anybody. Everyone voted his own convictions. I certainly don't think Governor Brown should have gotten all of the criticism he has received as a result of the Los Angeles convention."

Did he not feel a pang at not supporting his long-time friend and law partner, Governor Stevenson?

"No," said the Postmaster General decisively. "I would have been happy to support Adlai Stevenson had he announced as a candidate. But he did not. I felt I wanted to support someone who was actively a candidate. And, from my first meeting with Senator Kennedy, I was deeply impressed with him. I liked the authoritative way he answered tough political questions. It was apparent that he had done his homework. It seemed to me that he was well qualified to be President."

After the election, Day had "not the slightest inkling that I was being considered" for a Cabinet post, he said. But when President-Elect Kennedy, troubled by the vast postal deficits and seeking an outstanding businessman for the post, invited him to join the Cabinet as Postmaster General, he promptly accepted—even though it means he is now receiving about one-third the pay he used to receive.

When Day's selection was announced, one of his Illinois friends, Political Columnist Milburn P. Akers of the Chicago *Sun-Times*, wrote an enthusiastic column about him. "He predicted I'd do such a good job as Postmaster General that President Kennedy would give me something 'better,' " chuckled Day. "Actually, being Postmaster General is a job big enough to test the ability of any man."

Postmaster General Day grinned. "I saw a supposedly serious newspaper write-up on the new Cabinet," he said.

144

"According to the list, it contains two Republicans, three former governors, three experts, one businessman and one brother. According to this list, I was the businessman," Mr. Day chuckled. "I wonder what Defense Secretary Bob McNamara would think about that if he heard it? He was President of the Ford Motor Company."

The writers asked the Postmaster General to comment on the operations of the Postal Service. "What's wrong? Why is the department always losing money?"

"There are many differences between the Post Office and a business organized for profit," Postmaster General Day responded. "Take the rural delivery routes as one good example. On some routes, there are as few as two families per mile. A private business, operating purely for profit, could not undertake to serve such routes. We must do so. For many a small town," he added, "the post office is its main basis for identity.

"Not many people know it," Mr. Day went on, "but the Post Office does a great many things besides deliver the mails. For example, we have the task of registering some three million alien residents in the United States every year. We sell stamps for duck hunting. We carry and deliver local county newspapers. We have free mail service for the blind. We carry mails at a reduced rate for church and charitable organizations."

My Day smiled and toyed with a pen on his desk. "The Post Office Department now handles 65 *billion* pieces of mail a year. To give you an idea of how vast this figure is, consider that it is about 361 pieces of mail for every man, woman and child in America—or a number greater than the total number of *seconds* that have ticked by since Julius Caesar was alive.

"Some people have said that the British postal system is faster than ours. They tell us that in London, it is possible to mail a letter in the morning and have the addressee receive it in the afternoon. But the British postal system doesn't have to cope with the vast distances that we have in America. Furthermore, the New York Post Office alone handles far more letters than does the entire British postal system. And I hear that afternoon residential mail deliveries have just been ended in England.

"Also, Great Britain is no larger than our single state of Colorado. One of our biggest problems is distance. Another is congestion. It simply takes a considerable time to get across congested midtown Manhattan, for instance. Another of our

145

problems is the tremendous amount of mail put into the system from day to day. A single large mailing from a bank or business, for instance, may involve as many as a million pieces of mail. Literally tons of mail are put into the postal system by some direct-mailing companies."

The Postmaster General paused reflectively. "One term you never hear in the Post Office Department is 'junk mail,' " he said decisively. "Some people who aren't particularly interested in receiving such mail may consider it 'junk,' but many good, legitimate businesses stay in busniess on that type of mailing. It's a kind of business you don't have very much of in other countries. You might call it a symptom of the dynamic, aggressive American system of promoting business. The Post Office Department certainly doesn't have any intention of making any moves to stop this kind of merchandising. It isn't our intention to put any legitimate business out of business—especially not during a recession."

One part of the Post Office Department that operates at a profit, Mr. Day said, is the Dead Letter Office, where improperly addressed letters and envelopes wind up.

In the fiscal year 1960, more than twenty million letters were destroyed by the Dead Letter Office because they could not be delivered to the proper addresses. After a year in the Dead Letter Office, parcels are sold at auction and money is taken from the "dead" letters. This is turned over to the Treasury if not reclaimed within a year. The bonanza to the Treasury in fiscal 1960 amounted to $571,772.

Mention of the Dead Letter Office brought a smile to the Postmaster General's lips. He said that it reminded him of an experience of his own.

"When I was Vice President of Prudential, the Public Relations Department has a program whereby I sent autographed pictures of myself to managers of offices under my jurisdiction. I sent one autographed picture to a friend, signing it to him and adding, 'Best wishes . . . Ed Day.' The picture's frame was broken in the mails, but it was insured, so another was sent in its place and the incident was forgotten. Meanwhile, the first autographed picture was sent to the Dead Letter Office. When I became Postmaster General, a postal employee found my autographed picture in the debris, used ink eradicator to erase my friend's name, and displayed my autographed picture on his desk, saying: 'Best wishes . . . Ed Day.' " The Postmaster General chuckled. "I understand it caused quite a stir," he said.

146

Deputy Postmaster General of the United States
H. W. Brawley

For ten years prior to assuming his post, Mr. Brawley, 43, has been the Staff Director and Chief Clerk of the Committee on Post Office and Civil Service of the United States Senate. In 1953, he served as Executive Director of the Advisory Counsel to the Senate Post Office and Civil Service Committee, and is credited with directing intensive study at that time which resulted in major recommendations for improvement of the nation's postal service. These recommendations were incorporated into the Postal Policy Act of 1958, one of the more important recent laws improving the Postal System.

Assistant Postmaster General of the Bureau of Operations
Frederick C. Belen

Mr. Belen is a 47-year-old former Lansing, Michigan, lawyer. He has headed the staffs of four major permanent investigating committees of the House Committee since 1947. His studies are credited with savings of manpower and millions of dollars. Along with studies abroad in research on programs for mechanical mail handling, Belen has studied the use of machines for modernization of the postal system.

Assistant Postmaster General for Finance Ralph Nicholson

Mr. Nicholson is a specialist in management and financial operations. A University of Chicago graduate, who served on the staff of the former President of the University, Robert Hutchins, prior to service duty in World War II, Mr. Nicholson was the director and manager of the huge New York offices of Fuller & Smith & Ross Advertising Agency.

Assistant Postmaster General for the Bureau of Transportation
George O'Gorman

Mr. O'Gorman is a former American Express Company official. Forty-four-year-old O'Gorman heads one of the largest transportation operations in the world, operating a fleet of 85,000 motor vehicles in the postal service. It involves the expenditure of a half-billion dollars annually in moving the nation's 65 billion pieces of mail.

Assistant Postmaster General for Facilities
Robert J. Burkhardt

Mr. Burkhardt has the huge supervisory job of housekeeping for the nation's huge postal business. He majored in engineering studies at Purdue University and has had most of his business experience in the construction industry. His first job was as a timekeeper, from which he worked up to rodman, transit man, assistant superintendent and construction superintendent, before becoming the Vice President of Hudson Valley Aluminum Company of Newburgh, New York.

Assistant Postmaster General of the Bureau of Personnel Richard James Murphy

Mr. Murphy, 31, heads up the nation's largest civilian office force of 560,000 postal service employees. He is one of the youngest men ever to hold a sub-Cabinet post of such importance in the history of the Post Office Department. He majored in economics at the University of North Carolina and earned a Phi Beta Kappa key.

CHAPTER ELEVEN

Some Other Key Figures in the Administration

Director of the Budget David E. Bell

The tall, six-foot, four-and-a-half-inch, new Director of the Budget, David Bell, 41, like many of his colleagues in the Kennedy Administration is a Phi Beta Kappa. President Kennedy has described Budget Director Bell as "the man who says 'no.' "

He comes to his new post with unusual qualifications, including having been a Harvard University professor in the School of Public Administration. Mr. Bell also has had experience in the Bureau of the Budget and he once supervised a three-year mission to Pakistan as an adviser on economic planning and budgetary procedures.

Mr. Bell now heads the government office in which his government career began twenty years ago as junior analyst in the war organization section. He served in the Marine Corps as an intelligence officer during the war, then returned to the Bureau of the Budget as an examiner. In 1947, he became a Special White House Assistant and later Administrative Assistant to President Truman.

148

Mr. Bell heads an office with enormous importance in every phase of government. His staff numbers 450, his office annual budget is $5 million. He and his staff work closely with the Treasury Department, the Council of Economic Advisers, and other parts of the executive branch of the government in developing assumptions as to the economic and international conditions that in large measure determine the budget. The preparation and execution of the federal budget for any fiscal year covers about twenty-seven months.

The Budget Bureau's work is divided among five divisions and five offices. The divisions (Commerce and Finance, International, Labor and Welfare, Military, and Resources and Civil Works) do the ground work for the President's budget proposal to be transmitted to Congress as the federal government's annual work plan, keep under continuous review the financial obligations and expenditures of all agencies, and give attention to the level of economy and efficiency throughout the executive branch. The five offices are:

1. *Office of Accounting,* which improves accounting and financial management in the federal agencies.

2. *Office of Budget Review,* which develops general budgetary policies and assumptions, co-ordinates the review of agency estimates, and guides the preparation of the budget document, including the President's budget message.

3. *Office of Legislative Reference,* which provides co-ordination and clearance of agency views on proposed legislation, congressional enactments coming up for the President's signature, and drafts of executive orders and proclamations, all in relation to the President's program.

4. *Office of Management and Organization,* which concerns itself with preparation and execution of plans for improving the organization, management, and operating methods of the executive branch, dissemination among the federal agencies of information conducive to this end, and consultative assistance to them.

5. *Office of Statistical Standards,* which is engaged in planning and promoting the improvement and co-ordination of statistical information and statistical and report-collecting services in and for the federal government, including control over demands for information to be made on the public.

Briefly, here's how Director Bell and his staff determine how much money each of the myriad federal agencies should have in their budget:

Director Bell informs the federal agencies of the President's

149

budget policy, gives the larger agencies, after consultation with their heads, target figures or budgetary ceilings, and calls for estimates of appropriations. The call for estimates, containing detailed prescriptions for their presentation, goes out each June for the fiscal year beginning more than twelve months later (July 1).

Upon receipt of the Bureau's call, each agency's budget officer, as staff aide to the head of the agency, requests the chiefs of bureaus and divisions to submit their estimates to him. The extent and procedure of internal review are left to the individual agency, but scrutiny, from the lower levels to the highest, is usually extensive. By the end of September, the estimates and their justifications are before the Bureau.

Preliminary study of the estimates by the Bureau's budget examiners is followed by hearings for the individual federal agencies, held in the Bureau by staff teams of the divisions. The hearings, which may last more than a week for a large department, give opportunity for oral clarification by departmental representatives of all matters on which doubts have not been resolved by the written justifications. After each hearing, recommendations are formulated for discussion with the Director and a review group of his principal advisers.

The Director and his review group examine the recommendations made by the divisions. Because the proposed budget is not the product of the federal agencies but the President's, presentation of the estimates of the individual agencies, as revised after the previous hearing, is at this stage entrusted to each division.

When approved by Director Bell, the estimates, together with a highlight memorandum, are placed before the President for his consideration and sanction.

Early in January, the proposed budget, accompanied by his budget message, is transmitted by the President to Congress. The budget message, usually followed by a separate economic report from the President to Congress, outlines his financial program and its impact on the economic life of the nation. Next, the Appropriations Committee of the House of Representatives, acting through its subcommittees, studies the expenditure proposals in the light of such guidance as Congress may provide. The subcommittees hold hearings, taking testimony of officials and interested citizens.

Subcommittee recommendations are in the form of appropriation proposals supported by printed reports. These proposals reach the House through the Appropriations Committee for debate and action. The final appropriation, after Senate action, is sent to the President for his approval or veto, and then to the Director of the Budget for government apportionment.

Chairman of the Council of Economic Advisers
Walter W. Heller

Walter W. Heller, 45, former economist from the University of Minnesota, has served as an adviser on economic matters to this country as well as to governments abroad. He was also the economic adviser to former Governor Freeman of Minnesota, now Secretary of Agriculture. Dr. Heller is considered a man of "challenging ideas" and is generally regarded in the trade as a liberal. He has decribed himself as a "pragmatist"—willing to try to improve the economy by trying out new ideas and programs.

Professor Heller, along with Budget Director David Bell, usually attends Cabinet meetings. They influence the President and the whole course of policy-making decisions. Dr. Heller's position, while strictly an advisory one, makes him head of a task force designed to keep the nation prosperous. The recession and its accompanying unemployment are primary targets for the CEA. Long-range policies aimed at boosting the national economic rate of growth are also key objectives. The "balance of payments" deficit is another priority problem.

A tax expert, Dr. Heller has often advocated sweeping tax reforms as a means of stimulating the nation's productivity capacity and as a means of controlling inflation. His program is considered "visionary" by some conservative members of Congress, and foresighted by others.

He has stated he wants to lower the federal income tax rates from their present range of from 20 per cent in the bottom strata to the high of 90 per cent at the top. He has been quoted as saying that the present tax structure is inequitable, uneconomic, and stifles growth.

To speed up economic growth, Dr. Heller recommended and easing of the "tight money" policies of the Eisenhower Administration. This policy would lower interest rates, get money back into circulation and go a long way toward balancing the budget, he believes. To work at long-range programs for curbing unemployment, a better use of "human capital" is needed, Dr. Heller believes.

Education, knowledge and skills of individuals contribute as much to economic growth as does tangible "investment

151

capital" such as machinery and factories, he has stated. The chronically unemployed are usually the uneducated, non-skilled workers. Skilled labor jobs are usually available. It is the "human capital" (education and skill) that is lacking in the chronically unemployed. Professor Heller is also on record as favoring the "removal of the interest rate ceiling on federal long-term borrowing" to give the United States Treasury more flexibility in managing the public debt.

Professor Heller received his early education at Oberlin College and got his M.A. and Ph.D. degrees from the University of Wisconsin. He and his wife, the former Emily Johnson, a university professor's daughter, met in school and received their Doctorate degrees together. Hers was in psychology.

Housing and Home Finance Agency Administrator Robert C. Weaver

Dr. Weaver, a Harvard Ph.D., came to Washington from New York City, where he was Vice Chairman of the Housing and Redevelopment Board and one-time New York State Rent Administrator and Deputy State Housing Commissioner. He is a professional with wide experience in the field of housing. Citing the fact that 25 million Americans live in sub-standard housing across the nation, Dr. Weaver said, "I hope we'll be able to achieve real progress." He plans to develop a program through new proposals prepared by his staff of experts and by outside consultants to "work with all members of the Congress toward our common goal of better homes and better communities for all Americans."

Recently, President Kennedy sent a bill to Congress to authorize the formation of a new department of urban affairs to be headed by Dr. Weaver. If Congress approves, Dr. Weaver will be the first Negro ever to hold Cabinet office.

Dr. Weaver's policy of "open occupancy" in all federally subsidized housing was a factor in some opposition to his appointment. President Kennedy reiterated his trust in Dr. Weaver during swearing-in ceremonies at the White House. He said, "I have the highest confidence in Dr. Weaver's ability, his energy and his loyalty, and I am confident he will serve as a force in this important field for all America."

Dr. Weaver is a dedicated advocate of civil rights. He was the immediate past Chairman of the Board of the National Association for the Advancement of Colored People, a posi-

152

tion he resigned before taking up his post in Washington. During the hearings before the Robertson committee, Dr. Weaver was questioned closely regarding a speech he had made twenty-three years ago. The content of the speech was not up for question, but the group to whom he spoke was. The group was the National Negro Congress that was cited thirteen years later by the Attorney General as a Communist Front Organization. Dr. Weaver cited the fact that President Franklin Delano Roosevelt and the Republican Mayor of Philadelphia also participated in the meeting.

Dr. Weaver took a $1,500 salary cut in accepting the post. The government service record of Dr. Weaver is long. In 1933, he was appointed an Associate Adviser on Negro Affairs in the Department of the Interior, and a year later became an adviser on these problems in the department. He also served as a consultant on low-cost housing matters in the Public Works Administration during the depression years. He became the Special Assistant to the Administrator of the United States Housing Authority, working on federally aided public housing prior to World War II.

During the war, he held various posts and was mainly concerned with problems of Negroes. He was the Administrative assistant to Sidney Hillman of the National Defense Advisory Commission from 1940 to 1944, and worked simultaneously on the War Production Board and the War Manpower Commission of the Department of Labor.

Before going to New York, he served on the Mayor's Committee on Race Relations in Chicago and was a lecturer at Northwestern University. He later served on the faculty of Columbia University and New York University, and as a consultant to the Ford Foundation.

Dr. Weaver is married to the former Ella Haith, assistant professor of speech at Brooklyn College, and the couple has one son, Robert, Jr.

Three other professionals work with Dr. Weaver in running the housing agency. They are Neal J. Hardy, 46, who describes himself as a "careerist in housing" and who heads up the Federal Housing Administration; William L. Slayton, 44, holder of a Master's degree in Public Administration from the University of Chicago, who runs the Urban Renewal Administration; and Mrs. Marie C. McGuire, formerly the Executive Director of the San Antonio Housing Authority, who is in charge of the Public Housing Program.

Special Presidential Assistant John J. McCloy (Disarmament)

John J. McCloy was formerly the Assistant Secretary of War during World War II, and served as High Commissioner for Germany from 1949 to 1952. He retired as Chairman of the Board of Directors of the Chase National Bank before assuming his new post on President Kennedy's staff. He was at one time President of the International Bank for Reconstruction and Development.

Mr. McCloy is a graduate of Amherst and of the Harvard Law School. During World War I, he served in the A.E.F. in France as a captain in the field artillery. He was awarded the Distinguished Service Medal and is a grand officer of the Legion of Honor of France. He also holds the Order of Merit of Italy and the Grand Cross of the Order of Merit of Germany for services rendered in these countries.

Mr. McCloy, as is many another Kennedy appointee, is a Republican. But his achievements cross party lines. He has shown it in winning approbation from both sides of the aisle in Congress and without. He is a self-made man whose father died when he was only six years old, and he helped work his way through college waiting on tables. His assignment in the Kennedy Administration is to attempt to stimulate the lagging disarmament negotiations with Soviet Russia.

Special Presidential Assistant James Landis (Regulatory Agencies)

James Landis is the Special Presidential Assistant who "watchdogs" the federal regulatory agencies. A revamping is going on within the government now to revitalize these agencies, many of which the administration considers paralyzed by previous policies of appointing commission members who were unsympathetic with the laws they were supposed to administer. "We are aiming for a quiet revolution," the former Dean of the Harvard Law School has said. "We believe their proper functioning is essential to achieve the national economic growth we desire."

In recommending a wholesale shake-up and reorganization of the agencies, he has cited for special criticism the Federal Power Commission; the Federal Communications Commission; the Interstate Commerce Commission; the Civil Aeronautics Board; the Securities and Exchange Commission; the Federal Trade Commission; and the National Labor Relations Board.

154

The Tokyo-born, Princeton-educated Mr. Landis has been in and out of government for many years, and has been a member of several of the major regulatory agencies. He was on the Federal Trade Commission and was head of the Securities and Exchange Commission during the Roosevelt Administration. During World War II, he was head of the Office of Civilian Defense. He also directed American Economic Operations in the Middle East. He was head of the Civil Aeronautics Board until 1947.

Special Assistant to the President McGeorge Bundy (National Security Affairs)

The 41-year-old Mr. Bundy is a highly intellectual former Republican. He sits in a special category, working from the executive offices, but with direct access to the President and frequent liaison with the idea men on the Presidential White House staff. His function is to act as a go-between in the sensitive area of secret, security matters between the Departments of State and Defense and the President himself.

Born in Boston, Mr. Bundy was educated at Yale, where he turned in one of the most brilliant academic records ever achieved. At 30, he joined the Harvard University faculty. Four years later, he became Dean of the Faculty of Arts and Sciences, with a staff of more than 1,000, including 288 professors.

Although his original academic training was as a mathematician, Bundy's field has been foreign affairs. He has done research and written on foreign affairs for the Council of Foreign Affairs in New York, and collaborated with the late Secretary of War, Henry Stimson, on the latter's book, *On Active Service.* Bundy's father, interestingly, was an Assistant Secretary of State under President Herbert Hoover.

One of Bundy's primary jobs is in presiding over the National Security Council planning staff, which drafts long-range plans in the field of foreign policy and defense, vital to the security and "survivability" of the nation.

Special Presidential Assistant Kenneth O'Donnell

At 36, Mr. O'Donnell performs the duties of the Appointments Secretary for the President. He is considered an adviser, confidant and an assistant to the President, whom he has known and worked for over a ten-year period. He graduated from Harvard in 1949 and was a four-year letter man and halfback on the varsity football squad on which Robert

Kennedy played end. He holds a law degree from Boston College of Law.

Mr. O'Donnell was the administrative assistant to Robert Kennedy when the latter was Chief Counsel for the Senate Subcommittee investigating labor racketeering. He was recruited to the John Kennedy team in 1952 when the young Congressman from Massachusetts made his first bid for the Senate, and also worked on the astounding 1958 Kennedy Senatorial victory.

O'Donnell fits the picture of a "New Frontiersman" very well. He was an honor student and athlete at Harvard—which he attended as a scholarship student; he was a first lieutenant and war hero in the war, during which he flew thirty missions as a lead bombardier over European targets; he was shot down and wounded in a mission over Belgium, escaped and later received the Distinguished Flying Cross and the Air Medal with five clusters.

Special Presidential Assistant Theodore Sorenson

At 32, Mr. Sorenson is another long-time Kennedy man. He is considered to be one of the top members of the braintrust group aiding the President in policy-making decisions, speech-writing and research. He joined Mr. Kennedy's staff in 1952 as legislative assistant to the junior Senator from Massachusetts, studying bills, drafting memoranda, doing research and speech-writing—functions similar to those he now attends to on the staff of the President. Sorenson assisted Mr. Kennedy in the research on his book, *Profiles in Courage.*

Mr. Sorenson has a brilliant academic record. He is a graduate of the University of Nebraska Law School and a Phi Beta Kappa. He was first in his law class and editor-in-chief of the *Law Review.*

Mr. Sorenson is considered a selfless man, dedicated to President Kennedy. Some report that he is an "alter ego" to the President. His unofficial influence is believed considerable. As a Presidential adviser and assistant, he is a primary spokesman for the "liberal, intellectual point of view."

Special Presidential Assistant Lawrence O'Brien

Forty-four-year-old Mr. O'Brien is a veteran political organizer who has been on the Kennedy staff since 1952. He is the congressional liaison man on the Presidential staff. He is a lawyer who received his LL.B. from the Law School at

Northwestern University, though he is from the State of Massachusetts.

O'Brien, an executive in his own public relations firm in Boston at one time, has been active in organizing political campaigns since 1938. He was Director of Organization in the Democratic Congressional campaigns of 1946, 1948, and 1950, and was at one time the administrative assistant to Congressman Foster Furcolo, who later ran for and was elected Governor of Massachusetts. Mr. O'Brien played a key role in the 1952 campaign that pushed Congressman John Kennedy onto the national scene as a U. S. Senator, and directed the 1958 campaign for Mr. Kennedy's re-election.

Special Presidential Assistant Ralph Dungan

Mr. Dungan, 37, is another former Legislative Assistant to President Kennedy when he was in the Senate. His job is that of White House Staff Secretary, though he does not officially hold that title. His is a liaison, trouble-shooting job to see to it that the office runs smoothly. His past experience includes activity in the Bureau of the Budget, where he once served as a legislative reference assistant, then an assistant to the Director, and finally as an examiner of the foreign aid program. He was the Counsel to the Senate Labor Subcommittee for a brief time. He is a graduate of St. John's in Philadelphia and of Princeton University.

Special Presidential Assistant Fred Dutton, Jr.

Mr. Dutton is a Californian, formerly on Governor Edmund (Pat) Brown's staff. His most recent job was as Deputy National Chairman of the Citizens-for-Kennedy-Johnson movement in the election campaign of 1960. The 37-year-old Dutton is a graduate of Stanford University Law School. He once served as Counsel to the California State Judiciary Committee and later was chief assistant to the California Attorney General. His major assignment now is in the field of liaison with state governments, and department and agency heads of the federal government.

White House Physician Dr. Janet Travell

Dr. Travell, a handsome graying woman, is the first woman doctor to attend a President and the first civilian doctor to hold the White House medical post since the administration of President Warren G. Harding. (And even President Harding made his physician, Dr. Charles E. Sawyer, a brigadier general in the Army Reserve.)

Dr. Travell's job is to see to the health of the President. She also attends to the routine health care of the First Lady and young Caroline Kennedy. To satisfy both herself and the Secret Service in charge of the President's well-being wherever he goes, there goes Dr. Travell.

Dr. Travell is a general practitioner who has studied especially the pattern of muscular pain for years. She became the President's doctor after his serious spinal operation in 1955 and treated him for what she considered a condition of cramped back muscles. She has explained to the press that her treatments consisted of hot, moist packs, massage, which she still prescribes, and treatments of procaine injections. She is a strong advocate of regular exercise and has expressed the hope that the President will make regular use of the White House pool to keep in shape.

In her new job Dr. Travell and her top aide, Captain George Burkley of the Navy Medical Corps, look after the health of the five-hundred-member White House staff, including the Secret Service men, the valets, maids, secretaries, etc. The dispensary staff at the White House also includes two corpsmen and a nurse.

Administrative Assistant Timothy J. Reardon

Mr. Reardon, 45, is a Massachusetts man who graduated from Harvard in 1938. Before joining the staff of Congressman John Kennedy in 1946, he was in the advertising business. He has served longest on the President's staff. He was the Administrative Assistant for Mr. Kennedy in both the House and the Senate before taking over that responsibility in the Presidential office.

Reardon was the campaign co-ordinator for Mr. Kennedy in 1960 for the six New England states.

Special Assistant Jerome B. Wiesner (Science and Technology)

The former Massachusetts Institute of Technology research director is a scientist of note in the field of nuclear technology. He is considered an erudite, highly articulate spokesman who has the ability to communicate understanding of a complicated science in easily digested terms. His influence, because of the vast commitments of our national economy to defense and the maintenance of nuclear and missile weapons, is considerable.

Special Presidential Assistant Arthur Schlesinger, Jr. (Research and Special Projects)

The former Pulitzer Prize winner (for his historical work, *The Age of Jackson*) is the acknowledged head of the "brain trust" around the President. His job is broad in scope, including special missions for the President. He is a former Harvard professor, and has been jokingly referred to as the "court historian" of the present administration.

Press Secretary Pierre Salinger

The 35-year-old, cigar-smoking, former newspaperman once described himself as "a reporter for the rest of the press." He is the most publicized member of the President's staff because he deals with the press and is quoted on every hand by reporters looking for White House stories.

Salinger graduated from the University of San Francisco, then enlisted in the Navy. At 19, he was one of the youngest ensigns in the United States Navy. He was decorated for saving fourteen members of a patrol boat stranded off Okinawa in a 1945 typhoon. He was a reporter and night city editor of the San Francisco *Chronicle*. He was later with *Collier's* Magazine. While working on a rackets exposé story, he met Robert Kennedy and was persuaded to work for the McClellan Senate Subcommittee investigating labor-management relations. From there, he went to work for Senator Kennedy and became his press secretary.